"*The Governance Handbook for SEND and Inclusion* clearly and concisely
nent issues in SEND provision and inclusion so that governors can ask th
make the best decisions in the interests of learners with SEND."

— *Rebecca Howells, Chair of Govern...*

"I wish I had been given this book 30 years ago when I first became a school governor."

— *Fiona Millar, Journalist and Education Commentator*

"Professor Boddison has written what is undoubtedly the best practical guide to the governance of SEND in schools. Rich in content and clearly set out, there are 50 key messages to consider. The central exhortation for governors and school leaders to 'Think SEND' and embed 'Co-production' should be embraced by all."

— *Malcolm Reeve, National SEND leader: nasen (Whole School SEND)*

"This much needed handbook is an essential read not only for governors but for school leaders everywhere. The exhortation to 'Think SEND' resonates throughout each chapter as Prof Adam Boddison skilfully challenges misconceptions and orthodoxies, demystifies SEND processes and offers practical solutions and resources to ensure that the effective governance of SEND is rightfully placed at the heart of our education system."

— *Stephen Chamberlain, Chief Executive: Active Learning Trust*

"We all, as governors, have a responsibility for SEND students and this is a 'must read' for all board members. As a SEND governor at two schools/Trusts and as Chair of Governors at a special school, this book has been a huge reminder to me of my role. It has led me to checking my practice and the agendas of my meetings to ensure we pay due attention to the points raised in this book."

— *Jane Owens MBE, Chair of Trustees: Peninsula Multi-Academy Trust and Oak Trees Multi-Academy Trust*

"*The Governance Handbook for SEND and Inclusion* is essential reading for all governors. Not only does it place the needs of pupils with individual needs at the heart of governance, by its focus on the principle of 'Think SEND', it demonstrates good practice for effective governance across all schools and MATs. I will be adopting many of the strategies and techniques explored in this book, across our MAT in the coming months."

— *Michelle Prosser Haywood, MAT Strategic Lead — Safeguarding and Inclusion: University of Wolverhampton*

CN00539765

The Governance Handbook for SEND and Inclusion

The Governance Handbook for SEND and Inclusion supports governors and trustees in developing effective strategic practice to ensure an inclusive culture in their schools. Building on the six principles of effective governance, it provides useful tips on achieving the right balance of support and challenge so that schools are enabled to meet the needs of learners with SEND (Special Educational Needs and/or Disabilities).

Relevant for all governors and trustees across primary and secondary schools, multi-academy trusts and specialist settings, the book focuses on the role and expectations of governance in relation to SEND and inclusion. It includes:

- An introduction to SEND, inclusion and the six key features of effective governance
- Practical advice and guidance for SEND Governors and trustees on how to strategically monitor and review SEND provision
- A discussion of how the relationship between SENCOs, SEND Governors and Headteachers works in practice
- Advice on developing an inclusive culture in your school
- Sources of ongoing support and resources from professional organisations and websites.

This book will be beneficial to all education professionals working at a strategic level, including governors and trustees, school leaders and SENCOs. It recognises the central role that governors and trustees play in setting the inclusive ethos of a school and suggests ways to ensure that strategic practice is as effective as possible.

Adam Boddison is the Chief Executive Officer at the National Association for Special Educational Needs and Chair of the Whole School SEND consortium. He is a National Leader of Governance and trustee at two multi-academy trusts, spanning primary, secondary and specialist settings. Adam is a trustee of the Potential Trust and does regular board work as a Non-Executive Director. During his career, Adam was Director of the Centre for Professional Education at the University of Warwick and Academic Principal for IGGY (a global educational social network for gifted teenagers). He is a visiting professor at the University of Wolverhampton, a published author and a qualified clinical hypnotherapist.

@adamboddison

nasen

Helping Everyone Achieve

nasen is a professional membership association that supports all those who work with or care for children and young people with special and additional educational needs. Members include SENCOs, school leaders, governors/trustees, teachers, teaching assistants, support workers, other educationalists, students and families.

nasen supports its members through policy documents, peer-reviewed academic journals, its membership magazine *nasen Connect*, publications, professional development courses, regional networks and newsletters. Its website contains more current information such as responses to government consultations.

nasen's published documents are held in very high regard both in the UK and internationally.

For a full list of titles see: https://www.routledge.com/nasen-spotlight/book-series/FULNASEN

Other titles published in association with the National Association for Special Educational Needs (*nasen*):

Brilliant Ideas for Using ICT in the Inclusive Classroom, 2ed
Sally McKeown and Angela McGlashon
2015/pb: 978-1-138-80902-4

Curricula for Teaching Children and Young People with Severe or Profound and Multiple Learning Difficulties: Practical Strategies for Educational Professionals
Peter Imray and Viv Hinchcliffe
2013/pb: 978-0-415-83847-4

Time to Talk: Implementing Outstanding Practice in Speech, Language and Communication
Jean Gross
2013/pb: 978-0-415-63334-5

Promoting and Delivering School-to-School Support for Special Educational Needs: A Practical Guide for SENCOs
Rita Cheminais
2013/pb 978-0-415-63370-3

Dyslexia and Inclusion: Classroom Approaches for Assessment, Teaching and Learning, 2ed
Gavin Reid
2012/pb: 978-0-415-60758-2

The Equality Act for Educational Professionals: A Simple Guide to Disability and Inclusion in Schools
Geraldine Hills
2012/pb: 978-0-415-68768-3

Using Playful Practice to Communicate with Special Children
Margaret Corke
2012/pb: 978-0-415-68767-6

Language for Learning in the Secondary School: A Practical Guide for Supporting Students with Speech, Language and Communication Needs
Sue Hayden and Emma Jordan
2012/pb: 978-0-415-61975-2

The Governance Handbook for SEND and Inclusion

Schools that Work for All Learners

Adam Boddison

Routledge
Taylor & Francis Group
LONDON AND NEW YORK

First published 2021
by Routledge
2 Park Square, Milton Park, Abingdon, Oxon OX14 4RN

by Routledge
52 Vanderbilt Avenue, New York, NY 10017

Routledge is an imprint of the Taylor & Francis Group, an informa business

© 2021 Adam Boddison

The right of Adam Boddison to be identified as author of this work has been asserted by him in accordance with sections 77 and 78 of the Copyright, Designs and Patents Act 1988.

All rights reserved. No part of this book may be reprinted or reproduced or utilised in any form or by any electronic, mechanical, or other means, now known or hereafter invented, including photocopying and recording, or in any information storage or retrieval system, without permission in writing from the publishers.

Trademark notice: Product or corporate names may be trademarks or registered trademarks, and are used only for identification and explanation without intent to infringe.

British Library Cataloguing-in-Publication Data
A catalogue record for this book is available from the British Library

Library of Congress Cataloging-in-Publication Data
Names: Boddison, Adam, 1981- author.
Title: The governance handbook for SEND and inclusion : schools that work for all learners / Adam Boddison.
Description: Abingdon, Oxon ; New York, NY : Routledge, 2021. | Series: Nasen spotlight | Includes bibliographical references and index.
Identifiers: LCCN 2020037644 (print) | LCCN 2020037645 (ebook) | ISBN 9780367370015 (hardback) | ISBN 9780367370039 (paperback) | ISBN 9780429352317 (ebook)
Subjects: LCSH: Inclusive education--Great Britain. | Special education--Great Britain. | Children with disabilities--Education--Great Britain.
Classification: LCC LC1203.G7 B63 2021 (print) | LCC LC1203.G7 (ebook) | DDC 371.9/0460941–dc23
LC record available at https://lccn.loc.gov/2020037644
LC ebook record available at https://lccn.loc.gov/2020037645

ISBN: 978-0-367-37001-5 (hbk)
ISBN: 978-0-367-37003-9 (pbk)
ISBN: 978-0-429-35231-7 (ebk)

Typeset in Helvetica Neue LT Std
by KnowledgeWorks Global Ltd.

Contents

Foreword

Fiona Millar

I have been a school governor for almost 30 years, always of diverse and inclusive inner-city schools, but I am ashamed to say that after finishing this book, I realised that I still don't know enough about SEND and inclusion.

I suspect that I am not alone and that there are many reasons for this. When I first became a governor, this was a subject that was too rarely prioritised. Thankfully that has changed. But I imagine that, like many other governors, I have been lucky to work with committed and knowledgeable colleagues who have taken on the SEND Governor's role, challenging us and the school's leadership in such a way that we may have felt the finer details of policy, legislation, language and pupil needs were being ably dealt with elsewhere.

The law and SEND funding have also been reformed continuously over the last two decades, and, at times, it has been hard to grasp the complexity, especially when it comes to SEND budgets. But the changes haven't resonated with governors as forcefully as has been the case in other areas of school leadership and sadly aren't always interesting enough to my own profession, the media. Just think about the way newspapers gloat over stories about parental choice, school league tables and even exclusions, without taking the time to delve into the impact all of these policies can have on children with SEND and their families.

As Adam repeatedly reminds us in this book, there could and should be a similar relationship between governors and their accountability for SEND strategy as there is between governors and their pupil premium obligations. Yet one has been given much higher profile and importance by successive governments with obvious consequences. This could and should change because there are profound social, moral and philosophical issues for all of us in this area.

What do we mean by inclusion? Will that definition be the same for every school? How do we know that even though we may pride ourselves on being inclusive, some young people may not feel included? Are you sure your school isn't off rolling? How often do you hear the voices of the families of the SEND community? How many governors understand the difference between the medical approach to special educational needs or disability and the social model? I didn't but I do now, thanks to Adam's careful explanation.

This book isn't just about governor responsibilities, to do lists and audits. It is about values, ethos and ensuring that governing boards have a shared understanding of the culture they want to create. We all need to look beyond the volumes of data we are obliged to process, to the day-to-day personal experience of all students, the relationships they have with staff and how we receive qualitative evidence as well as the numbers. Above all, we need to constantly check that we have the confidence to value every young person and their unique qualities and needs in what is a punishing, competitive public arena where the last set of results and Ofsted inspections can destroy reputations and careers.

When I looked through my notes after finishing this book, I found that the point I kept returning to while reading Adam's book was 'whole governing body responsibility' and the appeal for us to 'Think SEND!' regardless of what issue we are considering.

We expect all teachers to be teachers of SEND and so all governors should be leaders of SEND. This is an issue of equity and aspiration for all. If you are opening this book now, you must know you care and want to know more. It will make challenging and thought provoking reading, so make sure everyone on your governing body has a copy too. I wish I had been given it 30 years ago.

Fiona Millar
Patron: *nasen*

1 An introduction to SEND and inclusion

A note from the author

Before this chapter begins in earnest, it is worth flagging some practical points. The language in relation to special educational needs and/or disabilities (SEND) and inclusion is complex, politically-charged and frequently changing. In general, the term SEND is used in this book, but occasionally other terms will be used too, such as special educational needs (SEN), learning differences or learning difficulties. Whilst there are definitional differences between these terms, please note that they have been used interchangeably for the purposes of this book. It is also worth being aware that there are many other terms for SEND in general use, such as additional learning needs, additional support needs and learning disabilities.

In relation to governance, this book generally uses the terminology of governors, schools and Headteachers, but many of the principles discussed apply equally to trustees, multi-academy trusts (MATs) and chief executive officers. Also, the book generally refers to the Special Educational Needs Coordinator (SENCO), but there are other equivalent job titles such as the Special Educational Needs and Disabilities Coordinator (SENDCO) or Inclusion Coordinator. The principles discussed for the SENCO role are also applicable to multi-school roles, such as Director of Inclusion.

In education, and particularly in SEND, there are a lot of acronyms. So a glossary of acronyms (Appendix 3) has been included at the end of the book. If you are completely new to education (or SEND), then you may find it useful to familiarise yourself with this in advance of reading the book.

At the time of writing this book, the Department for Education (DfE) is conducting a strategic review of SEND, which is likely to result in major policy changes at a national level. Alongside this book, the reader should ensure they are up-to-date with the latest developments in this area. The impact of COVID-19 has elongated the review, but the government has expressed its commitment to complete the review during 2021.

Lastly, a note on my personal and professional experience in relation to SEND as this will give you, as a reader, some sense of the basis on which the content of this book is drawn. I started my professional career as a secondary school mathematics teacher and then went on to teach at primary level and ending up as the Founding Director for the Centre for Professional Education at the University of Warwick with a teacher training leadership remit spanning the early years, primary and secondary phases.

My current substantive role is Chief Executive of the National Association for Special Educational Needs (*nasen*), which includes being the Chair of the *Whole School SEND* Consortium, the Chair of the *National SEND Reference Group* and sitting on a number of other SEND groups and committees. I am also a Director of the *Leading Learning SEND Community Interest Company*, which is the quality assurance body for providers of the masters-level National Award for SEN Coordination.

From a governance perspective, I am a National Leader of Governance for the DfE and have extensive experience of governance across primary, secondary and special schools. In addition to chairing school governing bodies, I have also been the nominated SEND Governor and have experience of being a trustee for small and large MATs.

This breadth and depth of experience spanning SEND, governance and education more broadly have provided me with what I hope are useful insights and my aim is to share them with you throughout this book. My thanks to the many friends and colleagues who have supported me on this fabulous journey.

What is SEND?

Introducing the concepts of SEND and inclusion is not as simple as it might first appear. There are various legal, political and practical definitions, but for many people their reference point is based on personal experience. It may be that a friend, a colleague or a relative has SEND or that they have SEND themselves. Alternatively, they may have built their knowledge of SEND from their professional work, from the news or from social media.

There is no right or wrong way to learn about SEND and inclusion, of course, but we should be mindful that the early information and experiences a person has are likely to shape their overall views and opinions. For example, let us consider two pupils with a vision impairment who each attended a different mainstream primary school. For one pupil, his/her experience may have been extremely positive whereby he/she felt wholly included as an equal and valued member of the school community. For the other pupil, his/her experience may have been less positive in that his/her school tried to meet his/her needs, but never quite got it right and so he/she never felt fully included as part of the school community.

In the first scenario, the pupil may later struggle to understand why all mainstream schools cannot meet the needs of children with a vision impairment, since school worked fine for them. In the second scenario, the pupil may later take the view that mainstream schools are just not equipped to meet low-incidence needs (needs that occur relatively rarely in comparison to other types of need). Whilst this example was based on pupils with a vision impairment, an equivalent argument could be made for other specific conditions or indeed for SEND more broadly.

Individuals' views about SEND will likely be shared amongst family and friendship groups where personal perspectives have the potential to be both powerful and convincing in shaping the opinions of other people. Too often, I have witnessed people make decisions or set policy on the basis of the experience of their friend with condition X or their family member with set of needs Y.

The point here is that SEND and inclusion are concepts that are determined not only by definition, but also by personal experience and by cultural influences. Whilst there may be some common areas of understanding, each of us will have different perspectives on SEND and inclusion. Indeed, there are some significant differences of opinion between those who would be considered experts in the field. From a governance perspective, it is important to have a diverse set of experiences and perspectives to draw from at board level alongside clear systems and processes rooted in good practice, so that an informed approach to strategic decision-making can be taken in relation to SEND and inclusion.

The legal definition of SEN is set out in Chapter 6, Part 3 of the Children and Families Act 2014 (Gov UK, 2014) as follows:

1. A child or young person has special educational needs if he or she has a learning difficulty or disability which calls for special educational provision to be made for him or her.
2. A child of compulsory school age or a young person has a learning difficulty or disability if he or she:
   (a) has a significantly greater difficulty in learning than the majority of others of the same age, or
   (b) has a disability which prevents or hinders him or her from making use of facilities of a kind generally provided for others of the same age in mainstream schools or mainstream post-16 institutions.
3. A child under compulsory school age has a learning difficulty or disability if he or she is likely to be within subsection (2) when of compulsory school age (or would be likely, if no special educational provision were made).
4. A child or young person does not have a learning difficulty or disability solely because the language (or form of language) in which he or she is or will be taught is different from a language (or form of language) which is or has been spoken at home.

An important observation about this definition is that it is based on comparisons and relative difficulties rather than absolute thresholds of need. As demonstrated in Figure 1.1, when determining whether or not a child has special educational needs, it is important to:

- compare one child with other children of the same age; and
- compare the provision that they need with the provision generally available for others of the same age.

According to this definition, determining whether or not a child or a young person has SEND has more to do with the provision they require and how well others of the same age are learning. This means that if there were two children with the same profile of needs, but in different contexts, the extent to which they have SEND and require specialist provision may be different in each case. The following three examples explore this concept in more depth.

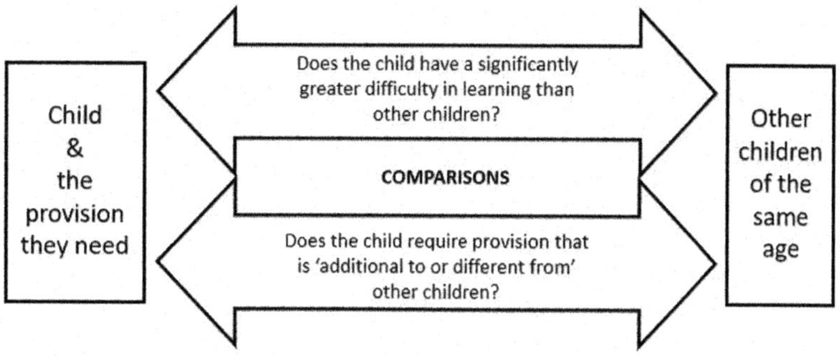

Figure 1.1 Comparisons to support the identification of SEND.

Example 1

Sarah and Cassie are both 15-year-olds and have autism spectrum disorder. They both struggle with sensory overload when classrooms or the wider school environment are too busy, too cluttered or too loud.

Sarah attends a large secondary school with more than 2000 pupils. Sarah's school believes in 'working wall' classroom displays as well as bright and engaging classroom environments. The SENCO has identified Sarah's sensory needs and that she does not always cope well with the school environment. Therefore, the SENCO has added Sarah to the SEN register and has made provision for her to be able to visit a low-sensory area of the school during break-time and lunchtime or whenever she needs to.

Cassie attends a small rural secondary school where there are only 230 pupils. Cassie's school has a curriculum based on nurture principles and the size of the school is such that the teachers are acutely aware of the needs of individual children. The school has a significant number of other children with a similar profile of sensory needs as Cassie and so they have taken the approach of classrooms being generally free of clutter with low-arousal wall displays as far as possible. Indeed, the smaller size of the school means it is likely to be calmer and quieter than a larger secondary school. The SENCO has not added Cassie to the SEN register because they have judged that her sensory needs are met by the wider approach of the school and so special educational provision is not required. It is perhaps useful to know here that the Children and Families Act 2014 defines 'special educational provision' as that which is 'additional to, or different from, that made generally for others of the same age'.

Sarah and Cassie have similar profiles of need, but their school environments are starkly different. The legal definition of SEN is such that Sarah may be deemed to have SEN, whilst Cassie may not. Furthermore, if Sarah and Cassie were to attend a different school, their SEN status may change despite their profile of needs remaining the same.

It is important to note that this example is not seeking to make a judgement about the approach of either school and there is no suggestion that one school is more inclusive than the other. The example seeks only to demonstrate that two children with a similar profile of needs can be identified differently and receive different types and levels of provision depending upon the wider context and physical environment.

Example 2

Ayyub and Samuel are both 12-year-olds and have complex needs. This means they have two or more severe needs that likely interact with and exacerbate each other. In some cases, this may include medical needs or life-limiting conditions. In the case of Ayyub and Samuel, their complex needs include both cerebral palsy and mental health needs.

Ayyub attends a special school where more than 80% of the pupils have a primary diagnosis of cerebral palsy and the school more generally specialises in provision for children with physical disabilities. The school uses a multi-disciplinary approach that brings together therapeutic interventions with medical care and quality teaching and learning. The relatively large proportion of children with cerebral palsy is such that the school is well equipped to meet the needs associated with this condition as a standard part of its day-to-day provision for all children. For Ayyub, this could mean that the school then places a particular emphasis on what additional therapeutic provision is required to support his mental health needs.

Samuel attends a special school that caters for a broader range of special educational needs and disabilities. The school groups children according to their primary area of need and they have decided to place Samuel in a small class of other children with social, emotional and mental health needs. The Headteacher at the school is confident that the standard day-to-day provision in Samuel's class will be effective in meeting his mental health needs. The focus in relation to the additional individual specialist provision is then on ensuring Samuel's cerebral palsy needs are also met.

As with the previous example, it is important to note that there is no judgement here about the approach of either school and there is no suggestion that one school is any more or less inclusive than the other. The point is that Ayyub and Samuel have a similar profile of complex needs, but the focus of the specialist provision is based on what is ordinarily available in their school as well as judgements about what their primary area of need may be. Special schools provide for a diverse range of needs and they may have a specialism around a particular need or cater for a broader set of needs. It is also true to say that two different special schools with similar profiles of needs amongst their pupil community may approach provision in significantly different ways.

Example 3

Zhang Li and Kwame are both 8-year-olds with a hearing impairment that makes it more difficult to hear what teachers, children and others are saying in a traditional classroom environment. Both children have used hearing aids since a young age.

Zhang Li attends her local mainstream primary school, who worked with the family to secure an Educational Health and Care (EHC) plan. The EHC plan recognises that the school is not able to meet Zhang Li's needs through its ordinarily available provision and so additional resource and specialist support have been provided by the Local Authority. In practice, this consists of support from a qualified Teacher of the Deaf as well as some 1:1 support from a teaching assistant, who is able to prepare in advance for particular learning activities. In addition to this, the school itself has invested in a programme to support both staff and children to learn British Sign Language.

Kwame attends his local mainstream primary school, which describes itself as a 'technology-enabled' school. Kwame does not have an EHC plan, since the Local Authority has assessed that his needs can be adequately met using the assistive technology available at his school. Specifically, the school has provided Kwame with a Bluetooth-enabled set of hearing aids that is linked to the school's audio-visual system. Every classroom has microphones built into the ceiling and Kwame can personalise/control the settings from his smartphone, which means he can independently hear teachers and other children.

Although Zhang Li and Kwame have similar needs, the level of special educational provision required is not the same because of differences in what is ordinarily available in each school. Zhang Li requires an EHC plan to access additional resource, but Kwame does not. An added complexity here is the extent to which hearing impairment could be considered to be a disability rather than a special educational need. Disability is a protected characteristic under the Equality Act (Gov UK, 2010) and so there would arguably be a requirement to put in place reasonable adjustments for Zhang Li and Kwame so that they are able to access and fully participate in education, without the need for an EHC plan. In practice, an EHC plan is sometimes seen as the mechanism to access the necessary resources to meet legislative expectations and to be inclusive.

In each of the three examples considered, the comparisons were between two pupils with similar needs attending the same type of school. Despite this, the extent to which the individual pupils were deemed to have SEN varied significantly and, therefore, the type and level of SEN provision also varied significantly. In reality, every pupil is different and every school is different, which is part of the reason why SEND is so complex and why it is impossible to have a one-size-fits-all approach. The resources and expertise available in a primary school may be very different to that available in a secondary school, a special school or an alternative provision setting. Similarly, the ethos, culture and values-base of a school will go some way in determining how resources are prioritised and allocated, which will in turn contribute to what is ordinarily available and what is not.

The principles established in these three examples are applicable to SEND more broadly and attention should be given to speech, language and communication needs and moderate learning difficulties as these are particularly prevalent in mainstream schools. Whilst the responses will vary from school to school, the ultimate indicator about whether an appropriate judgement about provision has been made is the progress of the child. Progress (in a broad sense – not just academic) is a universal measure of success that applies to all pupils in all settings.

Quality-first teaching

As the three examples demonstrated, a key factor when considering what special educational provision needs to be made is the ordinarily available provision. The better the quality of the ordinarily available provision (primarily teaching), the less special educational provision will need to be made. This principle is known as 'quality-first teaching' and it is essential if schools are to create a sustainable approach to SEND and inclusion. In summary, quality-first teaching is based on:

1. making sure high quality, inclusive provision/teaching is 'ordinarily available'; and
2. ensuring that the high quality inclusive provision/teaching is supported by sufficient additional specialist expertise.

Quality-first teaching will involve differentiation within the classroom and the SENCO has a key role to play in monitoring and supporting this across the school. One of the underpinning principles of quality-first teaching is the idea that what works for children with SEND often works for all children. In practice, this can reduce teacher workload in relation to lesson planning. The traditional approach would be to plan a lesson based on the majority of learners and then to adapt or add to it so it also meets the needs of those with SEND. An alternative approach would be to plan the lesson based on the needs of those with SEND on the basis it will then work for all learners. To be clear, this is not about reducing the academic level of the work, but rather about designing teaching and learning activities that are accessible to all pupils.

At a governance level, this principle still holds and is useful in the context of strategic decision-making. If a decision on school strategy is based on getting it right for the most vulnerable members of the school community, it is likely to be a decision that works for all learners. This is a more effective approach than setting a strategy that works for most learners, which then needs to be adapted so it can be implemented for the most vulnerable learners.

The social model of disability

The approach to SEND in England is moving from being based on a 'medical model' of disability to a 'social model' of disability. The medical model is premised on the concept that a person with SEND needs to be 'improved' or 'cured' through medical, social or educational interventions. The social model focuses more on the environmental barriers to participation and learning, and how these can be removed or reduced, including through wider societal change.

Models of disability – superpower example

Imagine a world where some people have the superpower of X-ray vision. If only 1% of people have X-ray vision, but Matthew is part of the 99% that do not have this superpower, would Matthew be considered to have a disability? Having asked this question a lot when speaking at various events and conferences, the general consensus is that because the vast majority of people do not have X-ray vision, then this is seen as 'typical' or 'normal', so the lack of X-ray vision would not be considered a disability. Indeed, some people said they would consider those with X-ray vision to be 'gifted' in some way as they are part of a small group of people who have an extraordinary talent or ability.

Now imagine a world where 99% of people have X-ray vision, but Matthew is in the 1% that do not. Would Matthew now be considered to have a disability? Again, the general consensus from asking this question on many occasions is that this scenario is somewhat different to the first. If the vast majority of people can do something that Matthew cannot do, many said they would consider this to be a disability.

This then begs the question as to what proportion of people in society need to have a particular ability for others to be considered to have a disability. The answers to this question are more diverse and a likely source of great philosophical debate, but that is (sadly) beyond the scope of this book. Returning to the main point about different models of disability, these invented superpower scenarios are useful in exploring the medical and social models, whilst minimising any preconceptions related to specific real-world disabilities.

In the two scenarios described here, Matthew's lack of X-ray vision is the same in both cases. Using the medical model of disability, a judgement would be made about whether Matthew has a disability based on a pre-determined set of criteria about Matthew's ability to use X-ray vision. This would be independent of the wider environment or the abilities of other people, so the same conclusion would be reached in each scenario. In practice, the medical model would not be applied in such a purist way because the criteria itself would be influenced by what is considered 'typical' and this may change over time.

The two scenarios fit better with the social model of disability than the medical model. Essentially, disability is determined more by the wider environment, which in this case was other people, than the specific profile of needs of an individual person. In practical terms, this is of critical importance, since it determines the approach we take to everyday life and therefore influences how inclusive we are as a society.

Extending the analogy further still, a world specifically designed to work for the 99% of people with X-ray vision is likely to inadvertently exclude the 1% who do not have X-ray vision. Conversely, a world designed to work for the 1% of people without X-ray vision would still work for those with X-ray vision and therefore include 100% of people. This demonstrates how getting it right for those with SEND will often work for all. It also demonstrates that people can be included by removing barriers in the environment rather than requiring the individual to change. For example, having a lift in a building removes an access barrier for a wheelchair user, but it is also useful for anybody who uses the building.

The social and medical models of disability can be applied to SEND more broadly as suggested in Figure 1.2.

Whilst the medical model and the social model of SEND are two distinctly different approaches, it is worth noting that this does not mean they cannot co-occur. England has been steadily moving towards the social model of SEND, but in practice there is a tendency to draw on both the

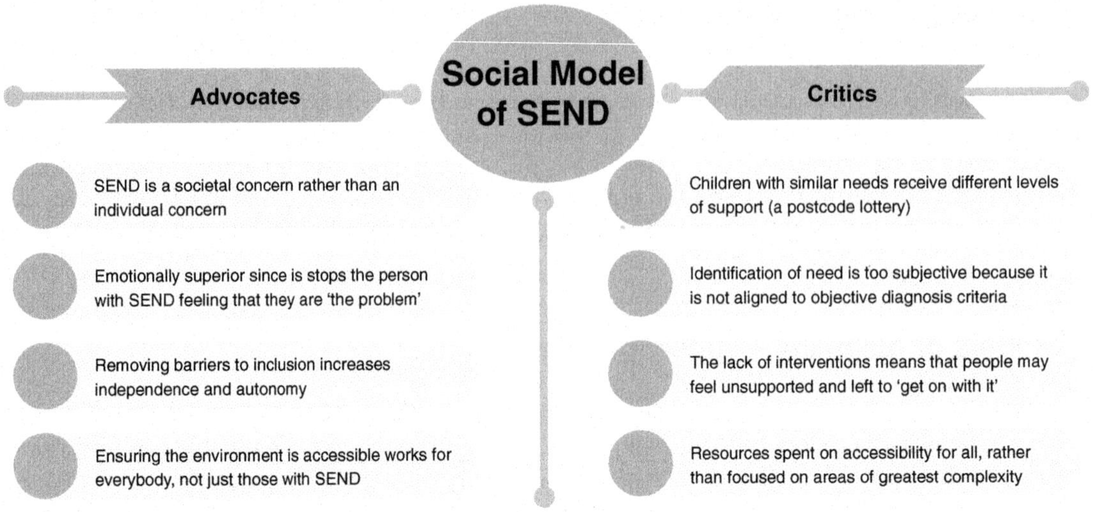

Figure 1.2 Advocates and critics of the social model of SEND.

Figure 1.3 Equality, equity and liberation (Maguire, 2016).

social and the medical model. This is sometimes described as the interactionist model and it recognises that people can be disabled by both social barriers and by their own physical/cognitive challenges (Tutt, 2016, p 9).

For example, if we consider attention deficit hyperactivity disorder (ADHD), the social approach in the classroom may involve breaking down learning into smaller chunks for all pupils in order to keep them better engaged. Conversely, the medical approach may involve cognitive behavioural therapy or actual medication, such as *Ritalin* or *Adderall*. For some children with ADHD, both a social and medical solution may be sought simultaneously.

The language of SEND is itself in transition between the medical model and the social model. Sometimes we talk about the diagnosis of SEND, but other times we talk about the identification of SEND. The term 'diagnosis' is rooted in the medical model of SEND and often results in a label of the individual's needs rather than an identification of the environmental barriers.

Part of the reason that the medical model has retained its prominence within schools is its more objective identification criteria, which makes it easier to make the case that a pupil has SEND. This in turn provides access to specialist services and support as well as enabling legal protections such as those enshrined within the Equality Act (Gov UK, 2010) and the United Nations Convention on the Rights of Persons with Disabilities (United Nations, 2006).

There are many variations of the image in Figure 1.3 that were based on the original 2012 version by Craig Froehle, a Business Professor at the University of Cincinnati. The image is incredibly powerful in demonstrating the affordances and constraints of the different philosophies of inclusion.

Comparing the 'equality' image and the 'equity' image is useful, particularly if we imagine the three crates to represent bundles of additional support or resource. The 'equality' image shows that allocating resource equally for every child helps some to have access but does not help others enough. Indeed, it could be argued that some are receiving additional support that was unnecessary and at the expense of others who needed the extra support.

Conversely, the 'equity' image shows a reallocation of the resource resulting in everybody having a similar level of accessibility. Critics of this approach may argue that it is unfair to withhold additional resource from those who already have access since they have as much right as others to reach their full potential. My argument would be that accessibility and potential are two different things. Additional resource may be needed for some at the individual level to ensure accessibility for all, but academic potential arguably has more to do with effective differentiation in the classroom. For example, low-threshold/high-ceiling tasks are by definition widely accessible, but some learners can take them further (differentiation by outcome). An example of such a task for a mathematics lesson is provided below.

Example of a low-threshold/high-ceiling task in mathematics

This problem is from the mathematics enrichment website www.nrich.maths.org and is called *Noah* (Nrich, 2020).

> Noah saw 12 legs walk by into the ark. How many creatures could he have seen? How many different answers can you find? Can you explain how you found out these answers?

Some pupils need additional support to materially access the problem, for example to accommodate literacy needs or motor skill needs affecting writing. However, from an educational perspective, the problem is widely accessible even to very young children. The website itself suggests a good preceding task would be to read the book *One is a Snail, Ten is a Crab – A Counting by Feet Book* (Sayre and Sayre, 2003), since this looks at adding different combinations of feet. For older or more advanced children, thinking about the number of combinations of answers, and whether or not they have them all, is a more complex problem.

Returning to the models of SEND, the 'equality' image is sometimes mistaken for representing the social model on the basis that resource has been used to support all of the children. However, this is a flawed interpretation since the social model of SEND is based on adapting the environment rather than providing individual support to every child. The 'liberation' image is a better representation of the social model of SEND, since it demonstrates how removing a barrier to learning (exemplified by the fence) the overall environment is improved and there is accessibility for all children.

Improving outcomes for pupils with SEND

In March 2020, the Education Endowment Foundation (EEF) published a report on SEN in mainstream schools (EEF, 2020). The report considered the strongest research available in relation to SEND and made five headline recommendations, which can be used by governors to challenge and support school leaders.

EEF recommendations for SEN in mainstream schools

The following recommendations are taken directly from the report (EEF, 2020, pp 8–9):

1. **Create a positive and supportive environment for all pupils without exception**
    - An inclusive school removes barriers to learning and participation, provides an education that is appropriate to pupils' needs, and promotes high standards and the fulfilment of potential for all pupils. Schools should:
        - promote positive relationships, active engagement and wellbeing for all pupils;
        - ensure all pupils can access the best possible teaching and
        - adopt a positive and proactive approach to behaviour, as described in the EEF's *Improving Behaviour in Schools* guidance report.
2. **Build an ongoing, holistic understanding of your pupils and their needs.**
    - Schools should aim to understand individual pupil's learning needs using the graduated approach of the 'assess, plan, do, review' approach.
    - Assessment should be regular and purposeful rather than a one-off event, and should seek input from parents and carers as well as the pupil themselves and specialist professionals.
    - Teachers need to feel empowered and trusted to use the information they collect to make a decision about the next steps for teaching that child.
3. **Ensure all pupils have access to high quality teaching.**
    - To a great extent, good teaching for pupils with SEND is good teaching for all.
    - Searching for a 'magic bullet' can distract teachers from the powerful strategies they often already possess.
    - The research suggests a group of teaching strategies that teachers should consider emphasising for pupils with SEND. Teachers should develop a repertoire of these strategies they can use flexibly in response to the needs of all pupils.
        - flexible grouping;
        - cognitive and metacognitive strategies;
        - explicit instruction;
        - using technology to support pupils with SEND and
        - scaffolding.

4. **Complement high quality teaching with carefully selected small-group and one-to-one interventions**
   - Small group and one-to-one interventions can be a powerful tool but must be used carefully. Ineffective use of interventions can create a barrier to the inclusion of pupils with SEND.
   - High quality teaching should reduce the need for extra support, but it is likely that some pupils will require high quality, structured, targeted interventions to make progress.
   - The intensity of intervention (from universal to targeted to specialist) should increase with need.
   - Interventions should be carefully targeted through identification and assessment of need.
   - Interventions should be applied using the principles of effective implementation described in the EEF's guidance report *Putting Evidence to Work: A School's Guide to Implementation*.
5. **Work effectively with teaching assistants.**
   - Effective deployment of teaching assistants (TAs) is critical. School leaders should pay careful attention to the roles of TAs and ensure they have a positive impact on pupils with SEND.
   - TAs should supplement, not replace, teaching from the classroom teacher.
   - The EEF's guidance report *Making Best Use of Teaching Assistants* provides detailed recommendations.

There are many schools where SEND provision is excellent and the needs of learners are well met. Unfortunately, this is not consistently the case in all schools. One of the ways in which the success of schools is measured is through academic outcomes. In some cases, schools with a larger proportion of children with SEND can feel that it is more difficult to achieve the same overall level of academic outcomes as schools with a lower proportion of children with SEND. In some instances, this leads to 'off-rolling', which is described as 'the practice of removing a pupil from the school roll without a formal, permanent exclusion or by encouraging a parent to remove their child from the school roll' (Ofsted, 2019).

In recent years, some school leaders have believed that they could maximise their academic outcomes by minimising the number of pupils with SEND on their roll. This was being done either by off-rolling or through exclusion at the point of admission. An example of the latter would be when a family is considering a potential school for their child, but they are advised that this is not the best school for them because there is another school that would be better equipped to meet their needs.

These attempts to 'game the system' were not always successful in improving academic outcomes at school level and this certainly created issues at a regional and national level. At school level, there was sometimes a fundamental misunderstanding about the academic potential of children with SEND. Whilst those with cognitive needs may find it harder to achieve the same academic outcomes as their peers, it is possible for them to achieve these outcomes when barriers are removed. There is also no reason why children with non-cognitive needs (e.g., physical disabilities, sensory impairments, communication needs or mental health needs) cannot achieve equivalent academic outcomes or even excel beyond their peers. In any case, outcomes are much broader than academic progress and attainment. To put this in context, families thinking about what outcomes they want for their children by the time they reach adulthood are likely go beyond academic exam results to include things like independence, friendship groups or happiness.

At a regional level, inclusive schools develop a reputation for being excellent at meeting individual needs and so they become *SEND magnets*. SEND magnet schools are more likely to become overwhelmed with the volume and complexity of need and are therefore at an increased risk of being unable to fulfil their inclusive ambitions. At a national level, there has historically been a concern about creating perverse incentives to over-identify the number of children with SEN due to having a direct link between identification and additional funding (Ofsted, 2010). Instead schools currently have a notional SEN budget as part of their core funding and they are expected to use this to provide for needs up to a certain threshold. This approach to funding is premised on needs being equitably distributed between local schools, which is unrealistic given the existence of *SEND magnet* schools and those schools trying to game the system. In practice, it means that inclusive schools become severely underfunded.

The problem of schools being penalised for being inclusive, both financially and through the various accountability frameworks, has been recognised at a national level (Boddison, 2019). Indeed, Ofsted's Education Inspection Framework includes a mechanism to ensure that no school can be judged as 'outstanding' unless they can also demonstrate that they are inclusive (Ofsted, 2019a). For these two reasons, it is essential that every school does its fair share in ensuring that pupils with SEND are appropriately provided for.

Ensuring that pupils are equipped with the skills to be successful and independent is as important as their academic outcomes. There is a whole chapter of the SEND Code of Practice dedicated to *Preparation for Adulthood from the earliest years*, which explores this in more depth (DfE and DoH, 2015, pp 120–140). Similarly, individual pupils will have outcomes and aspirations that are important to them personally. In addition to the outcomes that are measured by formal accountability frameworks, it is a moral imperative that a broader notion of outcomes directly aligned to the aspirations and needs of pupils is valued by school leaders and governors.

School exclusions

In discussing the proportion of children with SEND in our schools, it is important that we also consider the disproportionate number of fixed-term and permanent exclusions for this group. Data published by the DfE has consistently shown that for schools in England, children with SEND are seven times more likely to be excluded (DfE, 2019). Too often, it is the case that children are excluded for 'disruptive behaviour' instead of the behaviour being recognised as a communication of need. Governors must be confident that any exclusion is not a consequence of unmet needs and that the school has exhausted all possible forms of support and provision. Otherwise, the child is being penalised for the school's lack of effective provision and there is an increased likelihood of the decision being overturned. Governors should also be aware of the following government guidance related to excluding pupils with SEND (DfE, 2017):

- If a child is excluded because of their SEND, this may constitute a breach of the Equality Act (Gov UK, 2010). An allegation of discrimination could be referred to the First Tier Tribunal (SEND).
- Where there is a permanent exclusion, families can request an independent review of the decision. They can also request that there is an independent SEN expert on the panel as an expert witness at the school's expense.

A proactive step that schools can take in minimising school exclusions for children with SEND is effective identification of needs. It is common sense that the needs of a child can be better met once they have been identified. Unidentified needs are a significant factor in relation to permanent exclusion as demonstrated in the Timpson Review of School Exclusion (Timpson, 2019). The odds ratio diagram in Figure 1.4 was included in the report.

The bars in this diagram show how many more times likely it is that a child is permanently excluded if he/she has a particular type of SEN in comparison to a child with no SEN (represented by the horizontal line). If we consider the tallest four bars, it is not a surprise to see behavioural difficulties, emotional needs and mental health needs. However, it is perhaps more surprising to see 'no specialist assessment' and 'SEN type not recorded' with the latter as the group most likely to be permanently excluded. This suggests that unidentified needs can increase the risk of permanent exclusion. Governors can lay the foundation for making their schools more inclusive by focusing their support and challenge on ensuring there is effective identification of needs. This will also reduce the likelihood of fixed term and permanent exclusions for children with SEND.

The odds ratio diagram also highlights the stark difference between pupils who have an EHC plan and pupils who have SEND, but do not have an EHC plan. Having an EHC plan can provide an enhanced level of protection against permanent exclusion, but the lack of a plan does not change the responsibility of schools and Local Authorities to ensure that needs are met. The vast majority of pupils with SEND do not have an EHC plan, so governors need to be confident that effective identification is also in place for this group to minimise the risk of permanent exclusion.

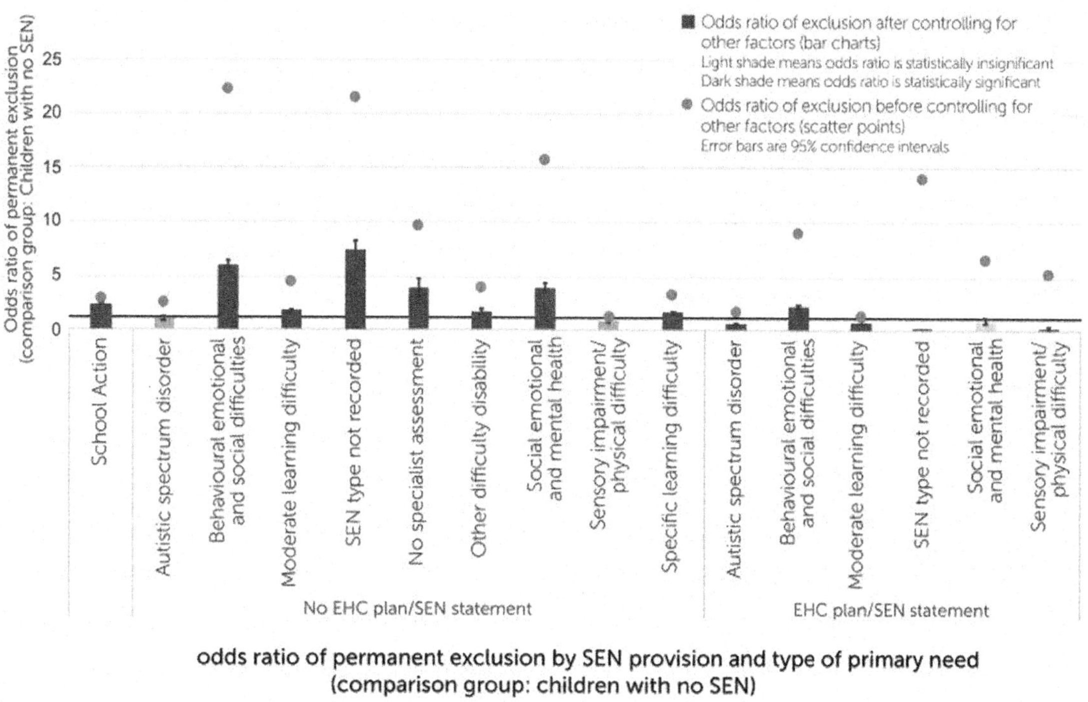

Figure 1.4 Odds ratio of permanent exclusion by primary area of need (Timpson, 2019).

SEND code of practice

Earlier in this chapter, reference was made to the Children and Families Act (Gov UK, 2014), which sets out the legal framework in relation to SEND in England. Section 77 of this Act sets out the requirement for the Secretary of State for Education to issue a code of practice with guidance in relation to the practical application of these duties. This guidance exists in the form of the SEND Code of Practice (DfE and DoH, 2015) and every leader and governor in your school should be familiar with this document. For governors, it is perhaps unreasonable to expect them to be familiar with all 292 pages of the SEND Code of Practice, but at the very least they ought to have a thorough understanding of Chapter 6, which is just 20 pages (Reeve and Packer, 2017). Some of this guidance for schools is discussed now, but some elements, such as the requirement for governing bodies to publish SEN Information Report, are covered later in the book.

There are lots of different categories of SEND, such as autism, dyslexia, ADHD, vision impairment, hearing impairment and physical disabilities. There are also many others that have not been listed here. It would be impractical and unreasonable to expect governors to know about every different type of need, but it is important that governors have at least a basic level of understanding of the broad areas of need. The SEND Code of Practice groups specific special educational needs and disabilities into four broad areas of need:

1. Communication and interaction needs
2. Cognition and learning needs
3. Social, emotional and mental health needs
4. Sensory and/or physical needs

Having a sense of the distribution of the four broad areas of need in your school is helpful for governors as it minimises the risk of considering pupils with SEND as one homogenous group when making strategic decisions. Further consideration will be given to how governors can practically use their knowledge of the profile of needs in their school in Chapter 5. In the meantime, it is worth reflecting on how the distribution of needs in your school compares to the national distributions from the 2020 census data as summarised in Figure 1.5 (DfE, 2020b).

There are currently two levels of SEND within schools in England: EHC plan level and SEN support level. It is likely that pupils with complex needs will have an EHC plan, which provides access to support and resources beyond that which is ordinarily available in the school. Around 20% of pupils with SEND (equivalent to about 3% of all pupils) will have an EHC plan. For

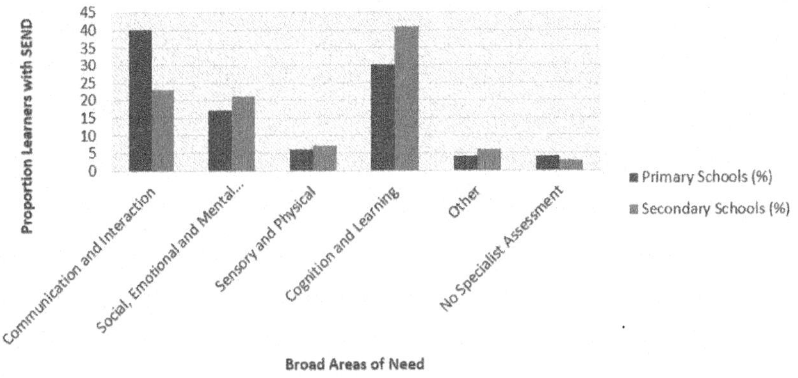

Figure 1.5 National distribution of the four broad areas of need, January 2020.

children in state-funded schools, just under half of those with EHC plans are in a special school, meaning that more than half are in mainstream schools.

Pupils with less complex needs are unlikely to have an EHC plan and will be at the SEN support level. Around 80% of pupils with SEND (equivalent to about 12% of all pupils) are at the SEN support level and the expectation is that their needs are typically met within the resources ordinarily available in the school.

The phrase 'ordinarily available in the school' has a level of subjectivity and will of course vary depending upon the school, the resources it has at its disposal and the additional support it can access via the Local Authority as summarised in Figure 1.6. The SEND Code of Practice (DfE and DoH, 2015, p 30) is clear that each Local Authority must publish what is known as the 'Local Offer', which includes details of how information, advice and support relating to SEND can be accessed and how it is resourced. The code goes on to specify that the aim of the Local Offer is 'to provide clear, comprehensive, accessible and up-to-date information about the available provision and how to access it' (DfE and DoH, 2015, p 59). A good Local Offer is a useful tool for families as it details what they can reasonably expect schools to provide, what can be provided through schools with the support of the Local Authority and what additional specialist services are available to support pupils with SEND. This is also a useful tool for governors as it provides a framework of expectations that can be used to facilitate effective support and challenge in relation to the SEND offer in the school.

The SEND Code of Practice (DfE and DoH, 2015, p 100) sets out how schools should use the structure of the 'graduated approach' to remove barriers to learning and to put effective special educational provision in place. A premise of the graduated approach is that there is a spectrum of need and for provision to be both effective and sustainable, it needs to be pitched at an appropriate level. The graduated approach shown in Figure 1.7 is a process that facilitates this, since it is cyclical and made up of four stages: assess, plan, do, review.

The following bullet-point list provides a useful summary and interpretation of what is expected at each stage, although it should be noted that there are some specific requirements that can be found within Chapter 6 of the SEND Code of Practice (DfE and DoH, 2015, pp 100–102). At every

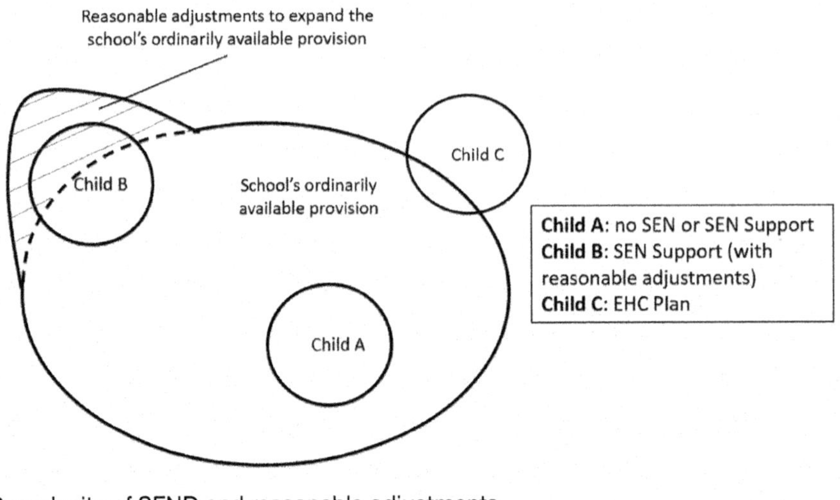

Figure 1.6 Complexity of SEND and reasonable adjustments.

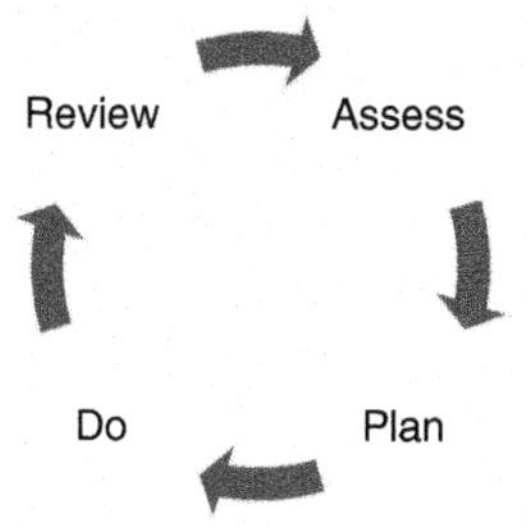

Figure 1.7 The graduated approach.

stage, it is important that pupils and their families are included as equal and meaningful partners. This is a key aspect of coproduction and is covered more fully later in this chapter.

- **Assess**
  - Identification of a possible special educational need:
    - Data shows that a pupil is making less progress or has slower development as compared to his/her peers.
    - Data shows that a pupil is making less progress or has slower development as compared to national data.
    - A pupil, his/her family, a teacher or another professional is concerned there may be a special educational need.
    - The provision available to a pupil is not meeting his/her specific needs.
    - The behaviour of a pupil is communicating that there may be an unmet special educational need.
  - Analysis of the impact of current provision:
    - Does the pupil have access to quality-first teaching?
    - Is the pupil, and his/her family, satisfied with the current provision?
    - What is the assessment of the class/subject teacher, the SENCO and other school-based professionals?
    - What advice has been received from external support services or from other specialists?
    - What interventions are currently in place? Are they effective?
- **Plan**
  - Working in partnership with pupils and their families, and deciding on what provision should be put in place to meet individual needs:
    - What adjustments, interventions and support should be put in place? What are the success criteria? How often will this provision (and its impact) be reviewed and how will it be monitored/recorded?
    - How do we ensure that all those who work with the pupil are aware of the provision and any role they may have in delivering it? Are there any additional resource requirements or staff training needs arising from this?
    - How can the support and provision at home and at school be aligned to have the maximum benefit for the pupil?
    - Is there a need to provide the pupil with SEN support?
    - Is there a need to request an assessment for an EHC plan? It should be noted that for an EHC plan to be issued, it may be necessary to demonstrate that a pupil's needs cannot be met within the resources typically available to the school. Therefore, it is likely that one or more cycles of the graduated approach will have been completed before requesting an assessment for an EHC plan.
- **Do**
  - Working in partnership with pupils and their families, and putting the agreed provision in place:
    - The SENCO will work with other school leaders (and governors if required) to deploy the necessary resource/staffing.
    - Discuss any implementation barriers with pupils and their families.
    - Update the SEN register (if required).
  - Ensure there is clarity in relation to professional responsibilities:
    - The class/subject teacher retains responsibility for the progress of all pupils in their class, irrespective of whether or not they have SEND.

        - Even when there is additional support in place (such as 1:1 support from a teaching assistant or external from a therapist), the class/subject teacher retains responsibility and accountability for the progress of the pupil. Teachers should ensure additional support is appropriately aligned to classroom teaching and that the overall provision is effective.
        - The SENCO may provide support or professional advice to the class/subject teacher, but it is the teacher who retains responsibility for individual pupils.
        - The SENCO is responsible for coordinating the overall approach to SEND provision in a school, the deployment of resources and the development of staff.
- **Review**
    - Working in partnership with pupils and their families, and assessing the effectiveness of the provision that has been put in place:
        - Ensure that provision is reviewed in line with the agreed timescales.
        - What is the quality of support and interventions? Is the provision effective? Has it resulted in the success criteria agreed at the planning stage?
        - If the provision is ineffective, how could it be improved? Is something additional/different needed?
        - What is the view of the pupil and their family? Have they had the opportunity to be part of the evaluation of the current provision?
        - Have the needs of the pupil changed?
        - What are the next steps?
    - Additional review requirements if a pupil has an EHC plan:
        - The Local Authority must review EHC plans at least annually. However, an early annual review can be requested (e.g., by the family or the school) if they feel the needs of a pupil have significantly changed.
        - The Local Authority can require schools to lead on elements the annual review process on its behalf.
        - Is the provision supporting the pupil to achieve the outcomes and ambitions clear and explicit within their EHC plan?

Whilst the graduated approach is often referred to as a cycle, it is probably more appropriate to think of it as an upward spiral. The idea is that with each iteration of 'assess, plan, do, review', the provision for pupils improves. Whilst the graduated approach has been developed as a framework to support learners with SEND, there is an argument that it could be used for all learners. Indeed, this is an example of the general principle that what works well for learners with SEND will often work well for all learners.

Whilst applying the graduated approach, it may become apparent that additional interventions or support are needed and, depending on the Local Offer, this may require an EHC plan to be in place to secure them. Each Local Authority will have a 'request to assess' process for EHC plans, and they will typically expect to see evidence that needs cannot be met at the level of SEN support. This is where excellent record keeping of how the graduated approach has been applied can prove invaluable. If an EHC plan is deemed necessary, the Local Authority must issue the final plan with 20 weeks of the 'request to assess'. Figure 1.8 provides a summary of the process and timescales once a 'request to assess' has been received.

It is a common misconception that Local Authorities fund the entirety of provision associated with an EHC plan. Although Local Authorities bear the full legal responsibility for ensuring that provision detailed in an EHC plan is delivered, schools may need to make a financial contribution from what is known as the 'SEN notional budget'. This is an amount of money that schools receive as part of the Dedicated Schools Grant, which is the main block of funding that most schools receive.

The SEN notional budget varies from school to school and it is intended to be used by the school to meet the needs of pupils with SEND. In practice, it is often absorbed within the wider school budget, so leaders and governors may not even be aware of the value of the SEN notional budget, let alone what it is spent on. Challenges can then arise once an EHC plan is issued because there is an expectation that the school will cover the first £6000 of provision from the SEN notional budget. There are two common key challenges:

1. If the SEN notional budget has been used for staffing costs as part of the wider school budget, it can be hard for schools to demonstrate that they are already spending the £6000 per year on a specific pupil.

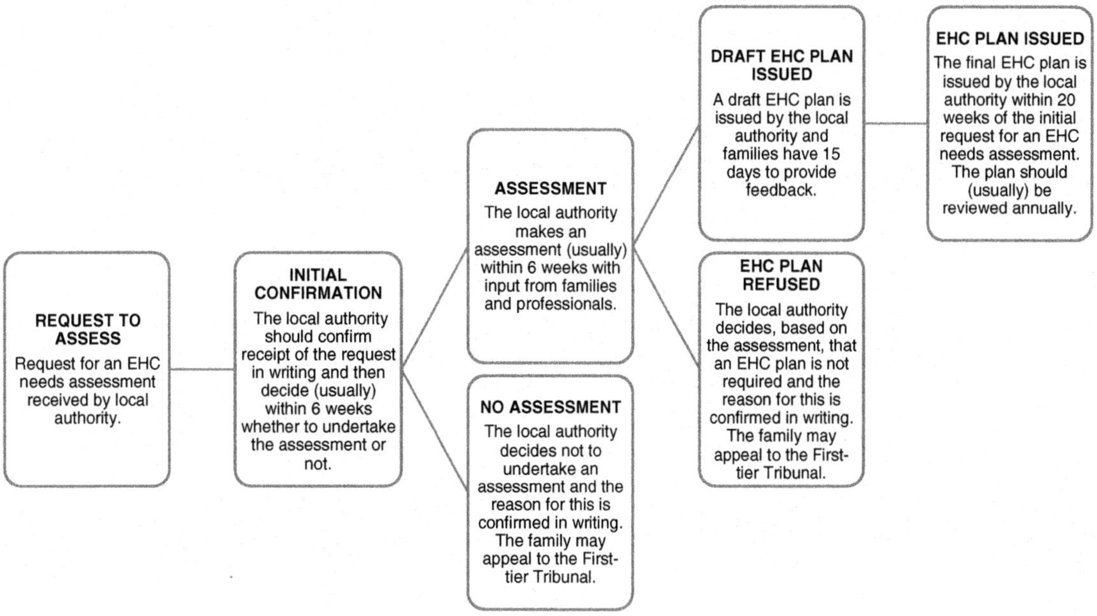

Figure 1.8 Summary of the process and timescales for a 'request to assess' for an EHC plan.

2. For some schools, the total size of the SEN notional budget does not cover the £6000 of funding per pupil with SEND per year that is needed.

In such circumstances, a positive and effective relationship between the school, the family and the Local Authority is essential in working towards a solution. The SEND reforms of 2014 were intended to encourage greater collaboration and joined-up thinking between education, health and social care, but this is still not happening consistently across all Local Authorities. There was also an intention to ensure that families and professionals worked together as equal and meaningful partners, which is known as coproduction.

Coproduction

One of the central aims of the Children and Families Act (Gov UK, 2014) was to ensure that services consistently placed children, young people and their parents/carers at the centre of the decision-making process. For families with children or young people with SEND, this includes ensuring there is a clear approach, which involves the participation of children and young people and their parents/carers in making decisions about how best to support their SEND at both individual and strategic levels.

Truly involving children, young people and parents/carers as equal and meaningful partners goes beyond tokenistic involvement or engagement and moves more towards genuine coproduction. From the school's perspective, the following three steps are sometimes used to describe their relationship with families as they move along the coproduction journey.

- Doing **to** families
- Doing **for** families
- Doing **with** families

Effective coproduction can bring many benefits both to the school and to the families involved. It recognises that parents/carers and pupils are equal and meaningful partners in the development and delivery of education, both individually and strategically. Their involvement is even more proactive, with their knowledge, skills and experience used to shape and make the services delivered more effective.

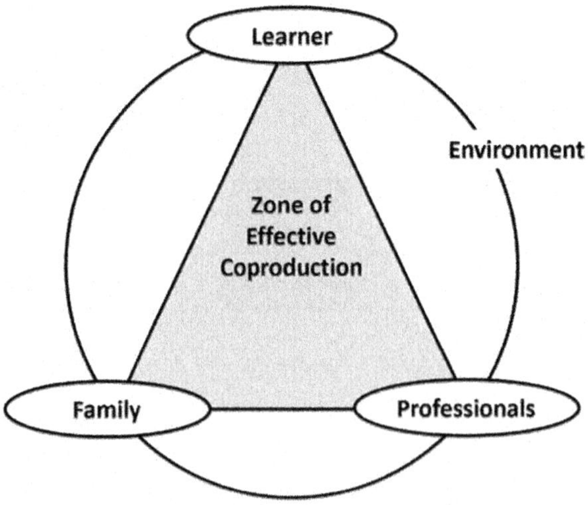

Figure 1.9 Zone of effective coproduction (Yates and Boddison, 2020, p 45).

It is argued that effective coproduction can take place at different levels (Yates and Boddison, 2020, p 44):

- At an individual level, for example within an assessment or review meeting.
- At a whole school level, for example with the development of a policy and approach on SEND.
- At a strategic level, for example in the development of a Local Authority-wide SEND strategy as part of the Local Offer.

This means that at a school or even Local Authority level, the views, wishes and feelings of children and young people and their families must form a central part of the process. Consideration should be given to where there may be barriers to coproduction so that these can be acknowledged and removed. For example, parents and carers may work long hours, shifts or have other working patterns which make it difficult to engage with teachers during the school's timeframe. Many schools are developing innovative approaches towards making it easier for parents and carers to engage with them, including the use of technology.

One of the central premises of coproduction in schools is that children and young people and their families could have skills that are complementary to the school offer. At its most effective, coproduction means equal partnership in a school where all resources on an issue are pooled together to provide the optimal solutions to a particular problem or issue, as indicated in Figure 1.9.

For schools thinking about where to start in relation to coproduction, it may be useful to consider the EEF guidance report *Working with Parents to Support Children's Learning* (Poortvliet et al, 2018), which recommends that schools do the following:

- Critically review how they work with parents and carers
- Provide practical strategies to support learning
- Tailor school communications to encourage positive dialogue about learning
- Offer more sustained and intensive support where needed

Inclusion

So far, this chapter has focused primarily on the legal definition and interpretation of SEND, but this sits within the wider context of inclusion. There is significant debate about what inclusion means in practice and how to define it, and this is a debate which has been going on for several decades. *The Warnock Report* (Warnock, 1978) is thought of, by educational professionals, as a significant historical landmark in relation to the current thinking about inclusion (Garner et al, 2019). Whilst *the Warnock Report* is often credited with coining the term inclusion (Devarakonda, 2013), Mary Warnock herself makes the point that the committee members responsible for the report had differing views about what the term inclusion meant (Warnock, 2019).

For many years, the debate about inclusive education has focused on *where* children with SEND should be taught (Purdy and Boddison, 2018). One of the central issues at the heart of this debate is whether special schools are inclusive on the basis that they are designed to provide for learners with complex needs, or non-inclusive on the basis they somehow discourage or prevent learners with complex needs from attending mainstream schools.

There are several international agreements, which some would suggest advocate the abolition of special schools (Rustemier, 2002), and the *Centre for Studies in Inclusive Education,* which commissioned Rustemier's original report, has more recently stated that 'special schools remain as a barrier to inclusion' (CSIE, 2018). The key international agreements most often cited for this argument include:

- The *United Nations Convention on the Rights of the Child* (United Nations, 1989), which states that a 'disabled child has effective access to and receives education [...] in a manner conducive to the child's achieving the fullest possible social integration and individual development'.
- The *Salamanca Statement* (UNESCO, 1994), which states that 'All educational policies [...] should stipulate that disabled children attend the neighbourhood school that would be attended if the child did not have a disability'.
- The *United Nations Convention on the Rights of Persons with Disabilities* (United Nations, 2006), which states that national governments 'shall ensure an inclusive education system at all levels' such that 'persons with disabilities are not excluded from the general education system on the basis of disability'.

On the other hand, there is the argument that the focus on the setting in which pupils are taught misinterprets the fundamental principle of inclusion, which has more to do with the interactions between learners and their school environment (Frederickson and Cline, 2009). This concept has been expertly explained by Rona Tutt (2016, p 9), who argues that inclusion is a process, not a place. The essence of her argument is that both special schools and mainstream schools can be inclusive or non-inclusive as a consequence of their actions, values and behaviours, rather than the legal status of their setting. Indeed, the argument made earlier in this chapter about 'SEND magnets' demonstrates the varying levels of inclusivity within the schools sector.

The current policy position in England is that pupils with SEND who wish to have their needs met in a particular mainstream school (or special school) can in theory secure this through having the school named on their EHC plan, since in this situation the school must admit the pupil, unless:

- the school would be unsuitable for the age, aptitude, ability or SEN type; or
- the attendance of the pupil at the school would be incompatible with the efficient education of others or the efficient use of resources.

In practice, both of these exceptions have proved extremely difficult (but not impossible) to justify, other than in situations where the named school or setting is clearly inappropriate, such as a 17-year-old learner requesting a place in an early years setting for example. In this case, the 17-year-old would neither meet the admissions criteria nor the DfE specification for the school.

The argument behind this approach is that it gives pupils and their families a choice, since they can attend either a specialist setting or a mainstream school depending on where the provision set out in their EHC plan can most appropriately be met. In my own professional role, I have heard critics of this approach argue that this is not a genuine choice since too many mainstream schools cannot meet the needs of learners with complex SEND.

Whilst inclusion is not generally about where pupils are taught, it is a factor that should be considered. For example, there is a general consensus that it would not be inclusive to have 100% of pupils with an EHC plan attending a special school, since this would constitute the complete segregation of learners with more complex SEND from the rest of the pupil population. It would mean that learners without SEND attending mainstream schools would have limited first-hand experience of complex SEND due to a lack of exposure, which could lead to misconceptions and the growth of unintended prejudice. This may also create additional challenges related to reintegration, for example when adults with or without SEND are living and working together later in life.

Conversely, it could be argued that having every pupil with an EHC plan attending a mainstream school is also not inclusive, since it may not have the resources and expertise to cater for complex needs. For example, if there are pupils who struggle with crowded environments

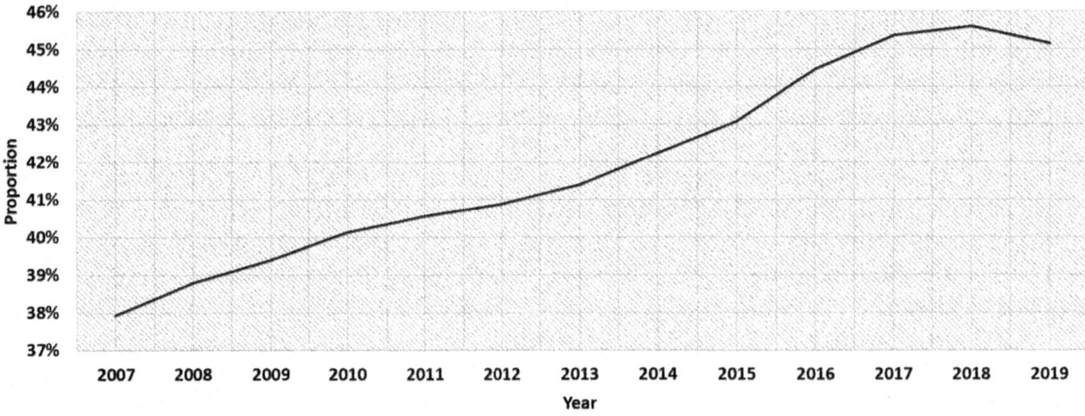

Figure 1.10 Proportion of learners with statements/EHC plans attending maintained or non-maintained special schools (DfE, 2007–2019).

as part of their profile of needs, a busy secondary school may find it far more difficult to meet their needs than a special school designed explicitly for this purpose. Similarly, some pupils with more complex SEND may require hoists to help them move around the school and this could be impractical and prohibitively expensive in a large mainstream school.

Increasingly, there are more nuanced and fluid approaches that avoid both of these extreme scenarios. For example, the growth in MATs with primary, secondary and specialist provision has meant that some pupils attend mainstream school as part of their week and access specialist provision as and when they need it. Similarly, there is the use of alternative provision as a temporary measure leading to reintegration back into mainstream school.

Some schools have an additionally resourced provision on their site, which is sometimes referred to as a 'SEND unit' or an 'enhanced provision'. The theory behind such an approach is that children with SEND who need more specialist provision can access this within the context of a mainstream school. When this is done well, it can be an effective way of including more children within mainstream schools, with a mixture of social and academic integration. However, the risk is that the additionally resourced provision becomes a segregated provision, even though it is located within a mainstream school.

The graph in Figure 1.10 shows how over time the proportion of learners with EHC plans attending a special school has increased from around 38% in 2007 to more than 45% by 2019. Given the consensus described above to avoid total segregation and the immediate impracticality of total integration within mainstream settings, this raises the question of what this proportion should look like.

The suggestion of a specific percentage would be problematic as it would likely be arbitrary and difficult to achieve in practice due to the dynamic nature of the national profile of needs. A good analogy would be the UK government ambition for 50% of all young people to attend university by 2010, a figure which had a limited, if any, evidence-base to support it (Turner, 2015, p 131). The government's social mobility ambitions are not being questioned here, but the fixed target is. Why should it not be 60% or 45% or 95%? The same criticism could be applied in relation to any target in relation to the proportion of learners with SEND attending a special school. An alternative might be to establish an acceptable banding to avoid the proportion getting disproportionately high or too low, but even this makes assumptions about learners and potentially creates unnecessary barriers to both inclusion and parental choice.

Another observation in Figure 1.10 is that more than half of learners with EHC plans have consistently attended mainstream schools. This sends a clear message to pupils and their families (and to schools themselves) that having an EHC plan is not in and of itself a barrier to attending a mainstream school.

Another analogy worth making at this point is one about grammar schools and selective schools more broadly. The argument often made about grammar schools is that they segregate a particular cohort of pupils from the mainstream school system. Depending on which line of argument is followed, this segregated cohort could consist of academically-able learners or of those from families with the financial, social and cultural capital to support them to meet the entry criteria. In either case, both grammar/selective schools and special schools are accused of segregating elements of the pupil population from mainstream schools.

The arguments for special schools and grammar/selective schools come from a similar place in that they are both based on the premise of meeting a more specialist set of individual needs.

Whilst this may be obvious, it is worth being explicit at this point that learners with SEND, including those with EHC plans, can and do attend schools that are academically selective. Data from the Independent Schools Council suggest there are more than 85,000 pupils with SEND in their schools and more than 4000 of them have EHC plans (ISC, 2020).

An education system without special schools and grammar/selective schools could be one where every pupil, irrespective of his/her needs or academic potential, attends his/her local mainstream school. Even accounting for the variation between mainstream schools, such an approach is arguably underpinned by the flawed concept of 'one-size-fits-all'. The idea that mainstream schools alone can meet the needs of every pupil no matter how diverse or complex is an admirable ideology, but is operationally challenging. The prevailing view from policy makers over recent years has been that an inclusive education system requires different types of schools and provision to meet the diverse range of needs that pupils have. On this basis, it could be argued that problems with inclusion do not arise because of the range of provision in the system, but because access to that provision is inequitable.

If inclusion is thought of as a set of values, rather than the physical space in which education occurs, we might ask why inclusion is not universal. One of the problems is the issue of unintended consequences of people trying to do the right thing. For example, if we consider the terminology associated with SEND, it is very easy to inadvertently use language that is outdated, inaccurate or that may cause offence. Therefore, some will choose to mitigate this risk by avoiding discussing SEND altogether, which can result in the person with SEND feeling alienated or excluded.

This is an effect seen at both at a systemic level and at a personal level. At a systemic level, if we consider Ofsted inspection reports for mainstream schools that have been published over the past decade, it can quickly be established that when SEND is referred to, it tends to be in a broad sense, for example making the point that overall provision is effective or not for a particular group of pupils. Less frequently is there a more in-depth account of the specialist provision. In discussions over time with a small number of inspectors (not a representative sample by any means!) about why this may be the case, several have shared their anxiety about unintentionally causing offence or about exposing a lack of expertise and confidence on a specialist area that they are expected to make a judgement on.

At an individual level, I would reflect for a moment on my own childhood in the late 1980s. Children are naturally curious about the world around them and I was no different. I remember being out shopping with my parents and seeing people with a visible form SEND, such as a physical disability, dwarfism or hyperactivity. Any child would instinctively be interested in and want to understand difference and diversity, but I was often told by my parents not to stare, since that would be rude. I imagine other children would have had similar experiences, where parents were seeking to do the right thing, but in doing so securing the opposite outcome from the one they were trying to achieve.

From the perspective of the person with SEND, this approach could mean that people regularly avoid making eye contact with them or interacting with them for fear of causing offence, so they can end up feeling isolated and lonely. Others with SEND may agree with my parents' view that the staring would make them feel uncomfortable, different and therefore excluded in a different way. This demonstrates some of the challenge and complexity of achieving inclusion in practice.

In the early 1990s, I went to see a theatre production, where the cast consisted of a high proportion of people with visible disabilities. On this occasion, nobody was telling me not to stare. Indeed, the opposite was true as I had come specifically to see the performance. It was an occasion where I was invited to look at people with disabilities for an extended period of time and to celebrate their theatrical expertise. After just a few minutes, the disabilities became unimportant as I was drawn into the performance itself. This is perhaps an indication of when we know that we have achieved true inclusion; when we can celebrate difference, but also see beyond it.

Sometimes, the pursuit of the perfect model for inclusion can itself be a barrier to inclusion. Instead of squabbling about the precise definition of inclusion, where the debate will no doubt continue for many years, it may be better to focus on the reduction of non-inclusive behaviours, where there is more consensus. There are some non-inclusive behaviours that are simply unacceptable or unethical, such as discrimination, bullying and off-rolling. Reducing these types of behaviours would shift the values-base of the education system firmly in the direction of inclusion. Indeed, it could be deemed that the direction of travel is more important than the final destination.

The reality is that there is no 'silver bullet' for achieving inclusion, since it is highly dependent on context and a complex weaving of ontological perspectives. Nevertheless, there are some principles of inclusion that have broad applicability. For example, a school that adopts an approach designed to support the needs of all its learners, rather than putting the needs of some ahead of the others, is surely one that is on the journey to inclusion.

Dual and multiple exceptionality

In providing an introduction to SEND and inclusion, it would be remiss not to consider the often-overlooked area of dual and multiple exceptionality (DME). There is sometimes a misconception that learners with SEND cannot also be academically gifted. Indeed, of the 13 primary categories of need used by the DfE in its annual census of pupils with SEND in schools in England, only three are cognitive indicators that the learner may not be academically gifted. In schools, this can have the effect of a learner with SEND being placed in a lower ability grouping, when it may not be appropriate. For example, a pupil with unidentified dyslexia needs may be placed in a lower academic group for English, but this is a consequence of unmet needs and not a true reflection of the pupil's academic potential in the subject. It may be that the pupil's needs are more appropriately met in a higher ability grouping when barriers to learning are removed. Indeed, there is a question about whether ability groupings are appropriate at all if quality-first teaching and effective SEND provision are in place.

SENCOs will no doubt be familiar with the term 'dual exceptionality' or co-morbidity where two special educational needs or disabilities interact with each other but are separate. Multiple exceptionality is where more than two special educational needs or disabilities interact. As shown in Figure 1.11, DME occurs where one of those educational needs is high learning potential (HLP), sometimes referred to in schools as 'gifted and talented'. DME is sometimes referred to as twice exceptional (2E), particularly in the USA.

In the *nasen*-commissioned publication, *Dual and Multiple Exceptionality: The Current State of Play*, the definition of DME is taken from one of the UK's leading academic researchers in this area, Professor Diane Montgomery (Ryan and Waterman, 2018, p 2). She gives the following definition:

> In the gifted education field, double or dual and multiple exceptionality (2E and DME) are terms used to describe those who are intellectually very able (gifted) or who have a talent (a special gift in a performance or skill area) and in addition to this, have a special educational need (SEN) such as dyslexia, or Asperger's syndrome.
>
> (Montgomery, 2015, p ix)

Many children or young people with SEND are achieving great things in school. Many have also been appropriately identified and are receiving the right support to meet their needs. Likewise, it is also recognised that many children with HLP are being supported to achieve the highest grades, whilst recognising that without appropriate support, they may not work to the level of their academic capabilities.

Nevertheless, a pupil with DME can face particular challenges with both their SEND *and* their HLP, which can result in chronic underachievement and low self-esteem. This can lead to a variety of issues such as school exclusion, self-exclusion, offending behaviour, poor mental health and related factors such as self-harm and suicide.

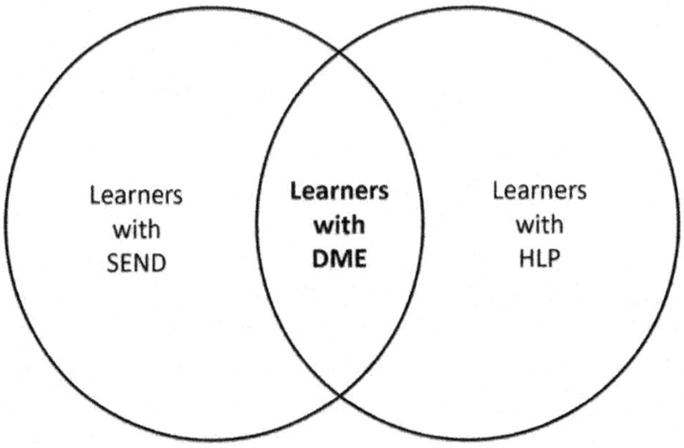

Figure 1.11 Dual and multiple exceptionality (Yates and Boddison, 2020, p 6).

Common challenges include

- Their strengths compensate for or even conceal a SEND, making it extremely difficult to identify correctly both the existence of or the extent of the issues faced by the pupil. Sometimes these can go unnoticed for years or even for a life-time.
- Their needs or abilities can be misdiagnosed or misinterpreted as something else, making it extremely difficult for professionals and families to provide the right support.
- Where a need is identified, emphasis can be placed on supporting this to the exclusion of the pupil's HLP, which also needs to be recognised and supported.
- Typical measures to support SEND may not be successful for a pupil who also has HLP.

One way of representing the different 'types' of DME can be seen in the matrix in Figure 1.12. The identification of the following four DME pupil profiles provides a useful outline to support a better understanding of the issues.

- **Type 1** – HLP recognised, SEND unrecognised: their ability enables them to 'get by', compensating for their SEND through use of their advanced abilities.
- **Type 2** – HLP unrecognised, SEND recognised: often labelled for what they cannot do, rather than what they can, often failing to achieve in school where they can display negative or disruptive behaviours.
- **Type 3** – HLP unrecognised, SEND unrecognised: each aspect masks the other. This is the group most at risk of under-achievement, since the needs are never addressed and the potential is never realised.
- **Type 4** – HLP recognised, SEND recognised: these pupils receive both the support and challenge they need.

Part of the approach to teaching children and young people with DME should be to move them to *Type 4* of the DME matrix so that both their SEND and HLP are recognised and supported, and they can receive an appropriate level of academic challenge and SEND provision.

According to Linda Silverman of the Gifted Development Center in the USA, in her book *Giftedness 101*:

> In most cases, their highly abstract reasoning enables 2E [DME] children to compensate sufficiently to get by with at least low average grades during their first years of school; but with each year level, their struggle intensifies. They must work harder to maintain passing grades.... Their gargantuan efforts are often rewarded by their being considered not good enough for gifted programmes and too good to qualify for accommodations. Catch 22!
>
> (Silverman, 2013)

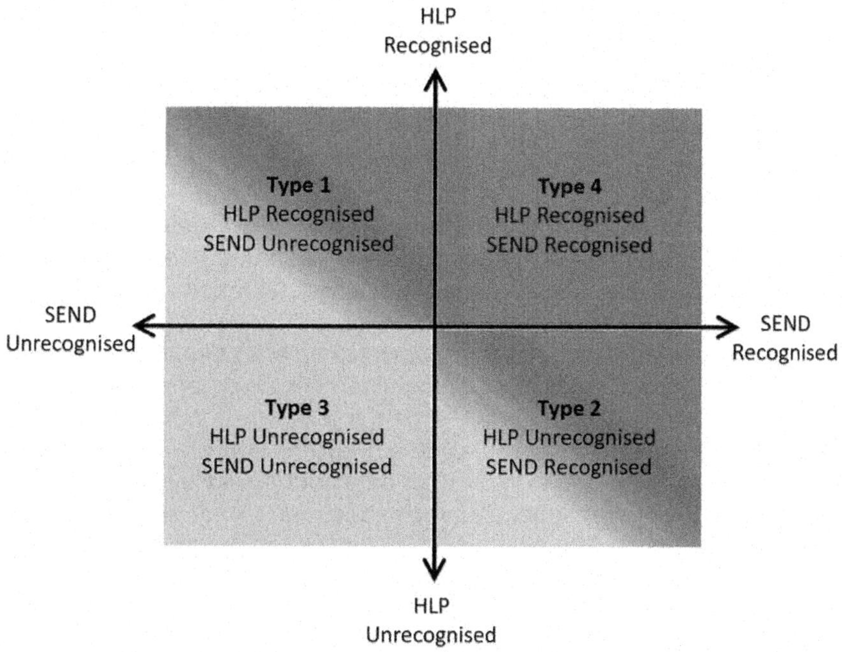

Figure 1.12 DME matrix.

Summary

This chapter has sought to provide a broad overview of SEND, which should be useful both for experienced governors and trustees as well as those who may be at the beginning of their governance journey. Having read this chapter, you should have now developed your knowledge and understanding of:

- The legal definition of SEND and some of the associated legislation
- Quality-first teaching
- The social and medical models of SEND
- Improving outcomes (e.g., academic and preparation for adulthood)
- Issues around school exclusions
- The SEND Code of Practice 2015, including the graduated approach
- EHC plans and SEN support
- EHC needs assessment process
- Coproduction
- Concepts of inclusion
- DME

The ten key messages that should be taken from this chapter are:

1. **The school environment is a key factor in the identification of SEND.** For two pupils with similar profiles of need, but attending different schools, one may be identified with SEND and one may not. One may require an EHC plan and one may have needs met at the level of SEN support through quality first teaching.
2. **The social model of SEND is focused on removing barriers to learning in the environment.** Whilst the medical model of SEND is focused on 'improving' the pupil, the social model of SEND is focused on making the environment more accessible.
3. **Effective practice for learners with SEND is often effective practice for all learners.** Rather than having a core approach to teaching and learning, which has to be adapted for learners with SEND, it can often be more appropriate, efficient and inclusive to have an approach that is designed for learners with SEND from the outset, since this will likely work for all learners.
4. **Value a broad notion of outcomes.** It is not just academic outcomes that are important. Schools need to ensure that they are preparing their pupils for adulthood and this should begin in the earliest years of education.
5. **Ensure that learners with SEND are not excluded from school because of behaviours due to unmet needs.** Pupils with SEND are seven times more likely to be excluded than pupils without SEND. Schools should seek to avoid excluding any pupils, but where this is unavoidable, it is important that all of the necessary provisions are in place, particularly if it is a pupil with SEND.
6. **The graduated approach of 'assess, plan, do, review' should be used to develop effective provision.** The SEND Code of Practice 2015 explains how the graduated approach should be applied and how it can help to gather the necessary evidence to feed into an EHC needs assessment.
7. **The vast majority of pupils with SEND are at the SEN support level.** Around 80% of pupils with SEND are at the SEN support level (around 12% of all pupils) compared to around 20% with EHC plans (around 3% of all pupils). Of those with EHC plans, more than half attend mainstream schools.
8. **Coproduction is essential for SEND provision to be effective.** Professionals and families must work in partnership as equal, meaningful partners in determining the nature of provision and how it is implemented.
9. **The concept of inclusion is complex and there is limited consensus on how it is achieved in practice.** There is significant debate about inclusion in schools, with much of it focused *where* pupils are taught (i.e., mainstream school or special school) rather than values and behaviours.
10. **SEND and HLP can co-occur and this is known as DME.** There is sometimes a misconception that pupils with SEND cannot also have significant academic ability (or HLP). When SEND and HLP co-occur, this is known as DME (or 2E).

2 Effective SEND governance

Chapter 1 introduced the concepts of SEND and inclusion. Chapter 2 will introduce the six key features of effective governance as defined by the Department for Education (DfE, 2019a):

1. Strategic leadership
2. Accountability
3. People
4. Structures
5. Compliance
6. Evaluation

These features will be considered in the specific context of SEND and inclusion with practical examples of how governance in this area can be strengthened at board level. This chapter will also explore the responsibilities of governors and trustees in relation to statutory policies, finance and strategic accountability.

The six key features of effective governance

In distinguishing the role that each of the key features has in relation to the overall aim of achieving effective governance, the Governance Handbook suggests that:

> The first two features are the core pillars of the board's role and purpose. The second two are about the way in which governance is organised, and the last two are about ensuring and improving the quality of governance.
>
> (DfE, 2019a)

It is useful at this stage to consider how this governance framework is operationalised in the context of SEND and inclusion. Table 2.1 provides a general overview of each key feature (taken from the Governance Handbook – DfE, 2019a) and makes suggestions as to what the role of individual governors and trustees, and the board as a whole might look like in each case.

It should be noted that the examples in Table 2.1, including individually named roles, are suggested responsibilities for effective SEND governance and not necessarily mandatory. There are three responsibility suggestions for the whole board and three responsibility suggestions for somebody within the board for each of the six key features of governance. However, every school or trust will be different, and the appropriateness of the suggested responsibilities will depend upon a range of factors, such as the school context and the governance journey to date.

The details provided in Table 2.1 are by no means exhaustive in covering all areas of governance responsibility for SEND and inclusion, but they offer a useful starting point. One approach would be for boards to review all the suggested responsibilities together to decide what they would like to focus on, what might be done differently and what additional areas of responsibility could be added. Some of the suggested responsibilities are discussed in more detail later in this chapter and in later chapters.

Before exploring some of these suggested responsibilities in further detail, it should be noted that there are other sources of similar advice worthy of consideration. For example, the *National Governance Association* (NGA, 2020) has a section on its website called the *Knowledge Centre*, within which there is an area dedicated to structure, roles and responsibilities. Another example would be the SEND Governance Review Guide (Rossiter, 2020), a peer and self-review tool, which suggests themes and areas that should be demonstrated by the board and the setting in general to support effective SEND governance. In Chapter 3, some guidance is given on how the SEND Governance Review Guide can be used as part of a wider review of SEND governance.

Table 2.1 Suggested board responsibilities for effective SEND governance.

		Suggested responsibilities	
Key feature	*Overview*	*Everybody on the board (All trustees/governors)*	*Somebody on the board (e.g., SEND Governor, chair, parent governor, safeguarding governor, clerk, etc.)*
Strategic leadership	Strategic leadership that sets and champions vision, ethos and strategy.	• Board members have a consistent understanding about what inclusion is and how it is realised within the school(s). • Board members proactively ensure there is a meaningful culture of coproduction. • Board members check that their decisions make their school(s) safer and more welcoming for pupils with SEND and that any unintended consequences are addressed.	• Ensure that SEND is built into the work of each committee (e.g., Committee chairs). • Check that risk assessment (or the risk register) informs strategic decision making to support the wider board responsibility of keeping pupils with SEND safe (e.g., board member responsible for health and safety or safeguarding). • Confirm the curriculum is accessible and works well for all pupils – this links directly to Ofsted's 'quality of education' judgement (e.g., chair of Standards Committee).
Accountability	Accountability that drives up educational standards and financial performance.	• Board members know how the attainment and progress for pupils with SEND compares with pupils without SEND and they make decisions to support school leaders in improving outcomes for all learners. • Board members consider the extent to which pupils with EHC plans are meeting their targets and provide an appropriate level of scrutiny on this. • Board members use an appropriate balance of support and challenge to ensure that accessibility is improving over time and that reasonable adjustments are in place and effective.	• Check that SEND is 'built-in' to all areas of the school development plan and not a 'bolt-on' (e.g., SEND Governor) • Understand the impact of the SEN notional budget and the impact of how school leaders have deployed other key SEN resources, such as the SENCO and any support staff (e.g., Finance Committee or Standards Committee). • Where appropriate, ensure that SEND and inclusion form part of performance management targets for school leaders (e.g. chair).
People	People with the right skills, experience, qualities and capacity.	• Board members ensure their own individual values align with the inclusive culture and wider ethos of their school(s). • Board members have direct experience of the offer for pupils with SEND and its effectiveness, e.g., through SEND Learning Walks. • Board members routinely review their own skills and experience in relation to SEND and inclusion, as well as developing their insights by considering the views of others in the school community including: o The confidence level of board members in relation to their knowledge and understanding of SEND and inclusion (as part of the governor/trustee skills audit). o The confidence level of staff in meeting the needs of pupils with SEND (as part of the staff survey). o The satisfaction levels of parents/carers about SEND provision (as part of the parent/carer survey). o The proportion of pupils who think the school is inclusive (as part of the pupil survey).	• Ensure there is an appropriate budget for governor (and staff) training, which can be used to develop a broad knowledge and understanding of SEND and inclusion (e.g., chair of Finance Committee). • There should be at least one governor who has (or is working rapidly towards) a more advanced level of knowledge, skills and understanding in relation to SEND and inclusion (e.g., SEND Governor). • It is important that SEND is a key part of the induction and onboarding process for new board members (e.g., clerk).

Structures	Structures that reinforce clearly defined roles and responsibilities.	• Board members adopt the principle of *Think SEND!* – this means that for every decision that is made, thought is given as to how it will impact pupils with SEND. • Board members give SEND the same status as pupil premium. • Board members maintain high aspirations for learners with SEND.	• There should be a SEND Governor and an Assistant SEND Governor to support effective succession planning (e.g., vice-chair). • The SEND Governor and the SENCO should meet at least termly (e.g., SEND Governor). • SEND and inclusion should form a regular part of discussions with school leaders (e.g., chair or vice-chair).
Compliance	Compliance with statutory and contractual requirements.	• Board members have a thorough understanding of how SEND provision at their school(s) is developing through their annual review of the SEN Information Report. • Board members are familiar with at least Chapter 6 of the SEND Code of Practice 2015. • Board members proactively ensure that discrimination is not occurring (e.g., ensuring that pupils are not excluded because of their SEND).	• **Local:** an understanding of relevant local compliance arrangements and processes, such as needs assessments, admissions, appeals, etc. (e.g., SEND Governor). • **National:** familiarity and compliance with key legislation, including the Children and Families Act 2014 and the Equality Act 2010 (e.g., SEND Governor). • **International:** awareness of international commitments, such as the Salamanca Statement 1994, the United Nations Convention on the Rights of the Child 1989, the United Nations Convention on the Rights of Persons with Disabilities 2006 and the United Nations Sustainable Development Goals 2030 (e.g., SEND Governor).
Evaluation	Evaluation to monitor and improve the quality and impact of governance.	• Board members review and refine the governance action plan annually using a process akin to the graduated approach. • Board members assess the impact of their governance on pupils with SEND through the systematic analysis of existing data sets (see Chapter 3). • Board members use a *SEND learning walk* (see Chapter 3) to inform and improve questions and discussions at future meetings.	• Visits to other schools or trusts facilitate benchmarking with other boards to identify areas for further governance development in relation to SEND and inclusion (e.g., chair). • There could be a periodic review of minutes to assess the balance of support and challenge in relation to SEND and inclusion – is the balance appropriate for the context? (e.g., clerk). • There could be an annual review of governor training (via a training log) to assess the impact training has had on the governance of SEND and inclusion (e.g., clerk).

Think SEND!

'Think SEND!' is one of the concepts outlined in Table 2.1 and it is designed to: (a) avoid unintended consequences of board decisions, and (b) ensure SEND remains the responsibility of all board members. Sometimes, boards will abdicate their general responsibilities for SEND because they feel they have a SEND Governor who has that responsibility. This can result in a situation where the wider board focuses their strategic decision-making on the 85% of pupils without SEND and the SEND Governor finds himself/herself a lone voice in making the case for the other 15%.

Having an individual role focused on SEND emphasises its importance, but this should be in addition to the general SEND responsibilities of the board, not instead of it. This is an issue that occurs at all levels of the system, not just at board level. Within schools, teachers will sometimes feel it is the role of the SENCO or a teaching assistant to be responsible for pupils with SEND, whilst they focus the rest of the children in their class. However, the SEND Code of Practice (DfE and DoH, 2015) is clear that every teacher is a teacher of pupils with SEND. Teachers are responsible for the progress and attainment of every pupil in the class, including those with SEND. The role of the SENCO, as the title suggests, is to coordinate provision and to be a source of more specialist advice and guidance. The same is true of the SEND Governor, who may or may not have expertise on SEND and inclusion, but this role is to support the wider board to discharge its duties rather than to take on the entire responsibility individually.

Similarly, at a political level, the appointment of a specific ministerial post (namely the Children's Minister) with responsibility for SEND brings with it the risk that the Secretary of State for Education delegates all SEND matters to that Minister rather than routinely considering SEND as part of wider decision-making. This potentially leads to a situation where the education system works for most children, but then has to be adapted to work for children with SEND. As discussed in Chapter 1, what works well for pupils with SEND is often effective for all pupils. Therefore, it makes sense to design an inclusive system from the outset, with SEND built-in to the decision-making process.

Within the Department for Education there are many different teams and units with different responsibilities. The existence of dedicated teams focused on SEND and inclusion again emphasises its importance, but it can allow other teams to feel they are 'off the hook' in terms of their own responsibilities for SEND and inclusion. Whether it is the teams responsible for assessment, curriculum or even school governance, all should have pupils with SEND built-in to their responsibilities rather than expecting SEND to be dealt with in isolation elsewhere in the department.

Whether it is governance boards, classroom teachers, school leaders, ministers or the Department for Education, the principle of 'Think SEND!' should apply in all cases. In practical terms, it involves proactively thinking about pupils with SEND in relation to every decision that is made. Returning to the context of governance boards, when strategic decisions are being made about anything, the board should take the time to reflect on how that decision will affect pupils with SEND. At the simplest level, this means asking whether it will improve or diminish their current experience. Most likely, it will affect different groups in different ways, but understanding this will be crucial in making decisions that are as inclusive as possible.

It is obvious to think about pupils with SEND for decisions where there is a direct contextual link, such as decisions about the financial resource allocated for teaching assistants or the introduction of a sensory room. However, 'Think SEND!' applies to all decisions, not just those that will overtly affect pupils with SEND. For example:

- Changing the timings of the school day
- Approving curriculum structure and content
- Amending policies, such as homework, behaviour or complaints
- Selecting providers, such as for a new website or grounds maintenance
- Agreeing staff:pupil ratios

It would be all too easy in the above examples to not consider the impact on pupils with SEND when making decisions, but all of them could impact on the inclusiveness of the school. If the principle of 'Think SEND!' is applied, it can empower boards to be more inclusive with their strategic decision making. This will save time and energy trying to fix a non-inclusive decision later on and will likely avoid parental complaints.

There are occasions when a difficult decision has to be made and even with the application of 'Think SEND!', there are unavoidable implications for pupils with SEND. The fact that this has been thought about in advance and is known at the point that the decision is being made allows the risks of such decisions to be mitigated. Boards may consider what other support or resources are available or whether there is something that can be adapted within the implementation to minimise any negative impact for pupils with SEND.

In Chapter 1, the importance of coproduction was emphasised and this is particularly valuable when difficult decisions have to be made. Families may bring ideas to the table that the board may not have come up with in isolation. Families can also bring a healthy dose of realism to the table about the potential impact of specific decisions on learners with SEND. Some situations could have more of an impact than the board had thought or in other areas the board may be being overly-cautious. In any case, coproduction only adds value to the principle of 'Think SEND!'.

Stakeholder perceptions of SEND and inclusion

Within the list of suggested governor responsibilities discussed earlier in this chapter, the importance of stakeholder perceptions was highlighted with an emphasis on:

- The confidence level of board members in relation to their knowledge and understanding of SEND and inclusion (as part of the governor/trustee skills audit);
- The confidence level of staff in meeting the needs of pupils with SEND (as part of the staff survey);
- The satisfaction levels of parents/carers about SEND provision (as part of the parent/carer survey);
- The proportion of pupils who think the school is inclusive (as part of the pupil survey).

Whilst these data sets are not a direct measure of inclusion, they are a useful proxy. Philosophically, it could be argued that a school is only as inclusive as those in the wider school community believe it is. Schools should routinely be undertaking governor/trustee skills audits and surveys of staff, pupils and parents/carers, so it should be relatively simple to add in any necessary additional questions in order to secure this perception data. Below are some sample questions/statements that you can use or adapt for your own school or trust:

- **Governor/trustee skills audit**
  - 1 = completely disagree, 2 = disagree, 3 = agree, 4 = completely agree
  - On a scale of 1–4, please indicate the extent to which you agree with the following statements:
    - I have sufficient knowledge and understanding of SEND and inclusion within my school/trust
    - I have sufficient knowledge and understanding of SEND and inclusion in general.
- **Staff survey**
  - 1 = not at all confident, 2 = not confident, 3 = confident, 4 = very confident
  - On a scale of 1–4, please indicate how confident you are that you can:
    - meet the needs of the pupils with SEND that you teach,
    - meet the needs of pupils with SEND in general.
- **Parent/carer survey**
  - 1 = completely dissatisfied, 2 = dissatisfied, 3 = satisfied, 4 = completely satisfied
  - On a scale of 1–4, please indicate how satisfied you are with provision for pupils with special educational needs or disabilities in our school/trust.
- **Pupil survey**
  - Do you think your school is inclusive[1]? Yes or No.

For the governor/trustee questions, it may appear from the wording that these are a measure of knowledge and understanding, but the answers will more likely reflect how confident board members are in relation to their own knowledge and understanding. The distinction between the two questions is also important as, for those who are not confident, it will determine whether the improvements involve providing more data and analysis from the school or securing more training and professional development.

In analysing the responses to these questions, considering the total proportion of governors/trustees who agree and completely agree (3 and 4) will allow analysis over time to provide an insight into the effectiveness of any improvement strategies that have been implemented. Comparing the results with other available data and your own knowledge of the board will help to identify under- or over-confidence.

For the staff survey questions, the analysis can be approached in a similar way to that described for the governor/trustee questions. The data will provide school leaders and SENCOs with an insight into whether any of the confidence issues relate to individual staff members or whether they are more general workforce confidence issues.

As with all the stakeholder groups, the responses are greatly enhanced by providing the opportunity for respondents to share examples that reflect their answers. Not only will this provide useful examples of what is working well so it can be maintained or scaled, but it also provides an insight into what targeted actions could lead to improvements. In the context of the staff questions, responses could directly inform the content of staff training, for example. A word of caution in relation to analysing confidence measures would be that sometimes confidence can decrease as knowledge, skills and understanding increase, since individuals begin to 'know what they don't know'. The qualitative examples will be helpful in identifying whether this is the case.

The questions for parents/carers and for pupils are designed to 'take the pulse' of the school's most important stakeholder groups. Again, analysing how the proportion of positive responses changes over time will indicate whether things are moving broadly in the right direction. The qualitative responses are essential here as there may be some issues that are beyond the school's control. Nevertheless, effective coproduction and child-centred provision are likely to have a significant influence on how children and their families respond.

At a governance level, having access to all these stakeholder datasets simultaneously can be extraordinarily insightful since they provide a multi-faceted set of perceptions in relation to SEND and inclusion. For example, consider the scenario where the staff survey suggests a high level of confidence in meeting the needs of pupils, but the parent/carer survey suggests there is dissatisfaction with SEND provision. This mismatch would indicate an issue in relation to coproduction, but it may also warrant further investigation to understand and address the discrepancy. In general, the board needs to be making strategic decisions that will lead to improving levels of confidence and satisfaction in relation to SEND and inclusion amongst all stakeholder groups.

The outcomes and insights from having undertaken a SEND learning walk or having conducted a review of SEND governance would provide further evidence to consider alongside the analysis of stakeholder perceptions. *Triangulation* is a strategy that involves looking for similarities of findings from multiple sources of evidence to enhance the rigour of the research and the validity of the conclusions (Robson, 2002, pp 174–175). In this case, boards should seek to triangulate findings from SEND learning walks, reviews of SEND governance and stakeholder perceptions. This will give a more valid evidence-base from which strategic decisions can be made. The practicalities of SEND learning walks and reviews of SEND governance will both be covered in more depth in Chapter 3.

Every leader a leader of SEND

The SEND Code of Practice (DfE and DoH, 2015) clearly established that SEND is everybody's responsibility and this principle is commonly referred to as 'every teacher a teacher of SEND'. A natural extension of this principle is the concept of 'every leader a leader of SEND' and it is argued by some that the latter is needed to achieve the former (Reeve, 2016; Boddison, 2018).

For classroom teachers, 'every teacher a teacher of SEND' includes ensuring that quality first teaching is universally available for all pupils and that the graduated approach is used to improve the effectiveness of provision. But it is perhaps less obvious how to put 'every leader a leader of SEND' into practice and not everybody will be convinced it is even necessary.

Some school leaders I have spoken to in recent years have questioned whether they need to be a 'leader of SEND' on the basis that they have a SENCO for exactly that purpose. Sometimes the analogy is used of school leaders not needing to be an expert in maths or a 'leader of maths' on the basis that there is a Head of Maths. The argument made is that the principles in place for the maths leadership analogy also apply to SEND leadership.

However, the reality is that these two situations are fundamentally different. SEND is not comparable to a subject area within the curriculum and a more appropriate analogy would be safeguarding. This analogy is more appropriate since it transcends subject areas and is focused on the fundamental needs of vulnerable children. Like SEND, safeguarding is everybody's responsibility. No effective school leader or governor would ever consider safeguarding to be somebody else's job. The fact that there is a designated safeguarding lead does not absolve leaders from their strategic leadership responsibilities in relation to safeguarding. Similarly, the fact there is a SENCO does not absolve leaders from their strategic leadership responsibilities in relation to SEND.

The idea that safeguarding is everybody's responsibility is not new (e.g., HM Government, 2006, p 48). However, in general terms safeguarding is more effective now than it was in the past. Historically, 'safeguarding is everybody's responsibility' was interpreted by some as them not needing to be overtly responsible because others were already taking the responsibility. This kind of approach risked children falling through the cracks and safeguarding not being as effective as it should be. The current situation in schools is somewhat different. It is now common practice that every member of the school community recognises they have a role to play in relation to safeguarding, and this supports the work of the designated safeguarding lead – it does not replace it.

This is precisely the positioning that we need in relation to SEND. All school leaders and all teachers should recognise that they have a central role to play in relation to identification and meeting the needs of pupils with SEND, and that this supports the work of the SENCO – it does not replace it. I am in no doubt that all school leaders would recognise the importance of safeguarding as a fundamental aspect of their role. Effective safeguarding is put in place to protect the pupils most at risk, but in practice it protects all pupils. Effective SEND provision is put in place to support pupils with SEND, but in practice it supports all pupils.

When 'every leader a leader of SEND' is referred to, it should be emphasised that this refers to leadership at all levels, including middle leaders, senior leaders, Headteachers, CEOs, governors and trustees. This is partly about leading by example, but primarily it is about leadership decisions that provide a culture of inclusion, which in turn enables classroom teachers to be more effective in meeting the needs of pupils with SEND. If universal provision is more inclusive and of higher quality, then fewer individual adaptations are needed. It is leaders who provide the framework within which universal provision sits; therefore we need every leader to be a leader of SEND.

Earlier in this chapter, it was suggested that one strategy for supporting the aim of 'every leader a leader of SEND' at board level is to give SEND the same status as pupil premium. To provide some context for this, in 2011 the pupil premium scheme was introduced by the British government as a mechanism of channeling significant amounts of additional school funding to close the attainment gaps for the most disadvantaged pupils.

Subsequently, Her Majesty's Chief Inspector (the then Head of Ofsted, Sir Michael Wilshaw) made his concerns clear on numerous occasions that pupil premium funding was not having the necessary impact on disadvantaged pupils (BBC, 2012; The Telegraph, 2013; The Telegraph, 2014). Similarly, a succession of reports published directly by Ofsted during the same period had a focus on the impact of pupil premium funding (Ofsted, 2012; Ofsted, 2013; Ofsted 2014). The net effect was that appropriate provision and outcomes for disadvantaged pupils became a high-stakes factor in relation to Ofsted's inspections of schools.

In order to assess the impact of the pupil premium, the government requires schools to publish an impact report annually, setting out how funding has been spent and what the impact was. This impact report is currently described by the government as a pupil premium strategy statement (DfE, 2019b), which must be approved by governors and published on the school's website. The length and details of the published strategy statement should reflect the overall size of the pupil premium allocation and should include the following information (DfE, 2019c):

- How much funding the school has been allocated this year
- How the school intends to spend the pupil premium
- The rationale for spending decisions, including the barriers to be to overcome
- The intended impact
- What impact last year's pupil premium spending had on pupils within the school

The direct involvement of governors in approving pupil premium strategy and impact statements means that the vast majority of governors are highly knowledgeable about the cohorts of disadvantaged pupils in their school, the provision in place for them and the impact of that provision. In contrast, my experience has been that governors are generally less knowledgeable about cohorts of pupils with SEND. Too many governors do not know the value of the SEN notional budget for their school nor do they know how much funding their school receives for pupils with EHC plans. Without knowing the value of the specific funding allocated to pupils with SEND, it is difficult for governors to assess the impact of this funding.

If Sir Michael Wilshaw's focus on disadvantaged students had also included learners with SEND, then pupil premium and SEND may have had an equivalent status in the board room. Instead, Ofsted's focus on pupil premium encouraged schools to prioritise disadvantaged students over pupils with SEND. Interestingly, the current Education Inspection Framework (Ofsted, 2019a) has significantly raised expectations in relation to SEND and inclusion in schools (Boddison, 2019).

In an overtly practical sense, governors looking to give SEND the same status as pupil premium could ask that the required strategy statement is extended so that it covers both SEND and pupil premium. This would provide governors with information to support them in holding school leaders to account for the provision and outcomes of pupils with SEND.

Governors should consider the overlap of pupils with SEND and those eligible for pupil premium, since these pupils are arguably double-disadvantaged and triple-funded. Double-disadvantaged in the sense that these pupils have SEND and come from a background of difficult socio-economic circumstances. Triple-funded in the sense that these pupils (taken as a whole group, rather than individually) receive the standard age-weighted school funding, pupil premium funding and an element of the SEN notional budget. For pupils with EHC plans, there may be additional targeted funding too.

It makes no sense to consider the pupil premium funded element of provision separately to the SEND funded element of provision. For individual pupils, the required outcomes are the same irrespective of the source of the funding. Therefore, school leaders should take a coordinated and more holistic approach to provision through an alignment of the different funding sources. At board level, governors should ensure funding is being used strategically and then seek to establish its cost-effectiveness and impact.

As discussed earlier, a key aspect of 'every leader a leader of SEND' is recognising that all board members have a responsibility in relation to SEND and not leaving the full burden of this to fall to the SEND Governor. To achieve this, it is useful to ensure that all board members exceed a baseline level of knowledge in relation to SEND. The SEND Code of Practice (DfE and DoH, 2015) is referred to extensively in this book, and it is recommended that both the SENCO and the SEND Governor are familiar with this lengthy, but important document.

In addition to Chapter 6 of the SEND Code of Practice (DfE and DoH, 2015), there are a number of statutory policies related to SEND and inclusion that governors should have in place and be familiar with because they have a particular relevance for pupils with SEND (DfE, 2020):

- Special educational needs and disability
- Equality information and objectives (public sector equality duty) statement for publication
- Accessibility plan
- Supporting pupils with medical conditions
- Behaviour principles written statement
- Admissions arrangements
- School exclusion
- Children with health needs who cannot attend school

This is not an exhaustive list of the relevant statutory policies, but it is a useful starting point. All of these policies should reflect the school's overall approach to SEND and their ethos of inclusion. To be clear, this is not about duplicating wording across policies because they are covering different aspects of school provision, but the policies do need to work well together without contradictions. To use a musical analogy, the SEND and inclusion messages of these policies need not work in unison, but they should work in harmony.

At a national level, the SEND Code of Practice (DfE and DoH, 2015), the Equality Act (Gov UK, 2010) and the Children and Families Act (Gov UK, 2014) are three key pieces of legislation. The legal duties in relation to SEND are set out in the Children and Families Act (Gov UK, 2014) and the statutory guidance of the SEND Code of Practice (2015). However, schools and trusts must also have regard to the duties set out in the Equality Act (Gov UK, 2010). For trusts, the requirement to adhere to these expectations may be set out as part of their funding agreements. The SEND Code of Practice (DfE and DoH, 2015) was discussed in more detail in Chapter 1, so it will not be covered again here. However, a summary of some of the key elements within the Equality Act (Gov UK, 2010) and the Children and Families Act (Gov UK, 2014) is included below (nasen and NGA, 2018). From a governance perspective, board members need to be satisfied that the school is adhering to both the letter and the spirit of this important legislation.

- **Equality Act 2010**
  - Schools must:
    - not discriminate against disabled pupils;
    - make reasonable adjustments;
    - publish an accessibility plan, which aims to:
      - increase the extent to which pupils can participate in the curriculum;
      - improve the physical environment of schools to enable disabled pupils to take better advantage of the education, benefits, facilities and services provided;
      - improve the availability of accessible information to disabled pupils.
  - It is unlawful for the responsible body of a school to discriminate (directly or indirectly) against, harass or victimise a pupil or potential pupil:
    - in relation to admissions;
    - in the way it provides education for pupils;
    - in the way it provides pupils access to any benefits or services;
    - in relation to school exclusions.
  - The 'reasonable adjustments' duty is an anticipatory duty:
    - where something a school does places a disabled pupil at a disadvantage compared to other pupils then the school must take reasonable steps to try and avoid that disadvantage;
    - schools are expected to provide an auxiliary aid or service for a disabled pupil when:
      - it is be reasonable to do so;
      - such an aid would alleviate any substantial disadvantage that the pupil faces in comparison to non-disabled pupils;
    - the duty extends to aspects of behaviour policies: for example if a pupil with autism may respond differently to behaviour expectations/sanctions than a pupil without autism, then schools should proactively take reasonable steps to ensure the pupil with autism is not disadvantaged;
    - 'blanket' policies or approaches where reasonable adjustments are not put in place in relation to SEND risk breaching the Equality Act (Gov UK, 2010).
- **Children and Families Act 2014**
  - Schools must:
    - co-operate with the Local Authority in reviewing local provision;
    - make sure that pupils with SEND get the support they need;
    - ensure that pupils with SEND engage in the activities of the school alongside pupils who do not have SEND;
    - inform parents when they are making special educational provision for a child;
    - ensure that arrangements are in place to support any pupils at the school with medical conditions;
    - have a clear approach to identifying and responding to SEND;
    - provide an annual report for parents on their child's progress;
    - ensure that the there is a qualified teacher in the role of SENCO;
    - determine their approach to using their resources to support the progress of pupils with SEND.

The box below includes five basic questions that it is reasonable to expect all governors/trustees to know the answers to in relation to SEND and inclusion (as an absolute minimum). Discussing these questions (and the answers!) at a board meeting will help to ensure that this is the case. Whilst these are perhaps basic questions, if every governor in England knew the answers for their particular context, then the national effectiveness of SEND governance would be in a stronger position than is currently the case.

Five key governance questions for SEND and inclusion

1. In our school, what is the distribution of the four broad areas of need as specified in the SEND Code of Practice (DfE and DoH, 2015)? How does this compare with national data?

2. What proportion of pupils at our school have EHC plans and what proportion are at the level of SEN support? Are our resources appropriately aligned to this?
3. What is the value of our SEN notional budget, what do we spend it on and what is the impact for pupils with SEND?
4. How are we realising our anticipatory duties in relation to 'reasonable adjustments' as per the Equality Act 2010?
5. Are we an inclusive school? How do we know?

The final question in this list about inclusivity is an essential question for senior leaders and governance professionals, since it is now embedded into the school accountability framework. Ofsted's Education Inspection Framework (Ofsted, 2019a) has an associated grading model that is cumulative rather than the previous approach of 'best fit'. In theory, this means that no school can access an outstanding grade unless they have first satisfied all of the 'good' criteria, which include:

- [Leaders] create an inclusive culture and do not allow gaming or off-rolling (Leadership and Management).
- Leaders adopt or construct a curriculum that is ambitious and designed to give all pupils, particularly disadvantaged pupils and including pupils with SEND, the knowledge and cultural capital they need to succeed in life. This is either the national curriculum or a curriculum of comparable breadth and ambition (Quality of Education).
- The curriculum is successfully adapted, designed or developed to be ambitious and meet the needs of pupils with SEND, developing their knowledge, skills and abilities to apply what they know and can do with increasing fluency and independence (Quality of Education).
- Pupils with SEND achieve the best possible outcomes (Quality of Education).
- There is demonstrable improvement in the behaviour and attendance of pupils who have particular needs (Behaviour and Attitudes).
- The school promotes equality of opportunity and diversity effectively. As a result, pupils understand, appreciate and respect difference in the world and its people... (Personal Development).
- [Pupils] show respect for the different protected characteristics as defined in law and no forms of discrimination are tolerated (Personal Development).

(Ofsted, 2019b)

There is also an outstanding grade descriptor within *Quality of Education*, which states 'Pupils with SEND achieve exceptionally well' (Ofsted, 2019b, p 49). This combination of grade descriptors sets out the clear principle that no school should be graded outstanding unless they can also demonstrate that they are inclusive (Boddison, 2019).

In addition to the above, Ofsted's school inspection handbook sets out a number of grade descriptors that could see a school graded as 'inadequate', including:

- The school is systematically gaming its results, entering pupils for courses that are not in their educational best interest (Leadership and Management).
- There is evidence that pupils have been removed from the school roll without a formal, permanent exclusion or by the school encouraging a parent to remove their child from the school roll, and leaders have taken insufficient action to address this (Leadership and Management).
- Pupils with SEND do not benefit from a good-quality education. Expectations of them are low, and their needs are not accurately identified, assessed or met (Quality of Education).
- Attendance is consistently low for all pupils or groups of pupils and shows little sign of sustained improvement (Behaviour and Attitudes).
- Incidents of bullying or prejudiced and discriminatory behaviour, both direct and indirect, are frequent (Behaviour and Attitudes).
- Pupils or groups of pupils are discriminated against, and the school is not taking effective action to address this (Personal Development).

(Ofsted, 2019b)

In addition to the moral imperative for school leaders and governors to be inclusive, the Ofsted accountability framework now formally recognises strong ethical leadership. However, it is still the case that school funding models remain a barrier to inclusion in some instances and this long-standing issue needs to be addressed.

SEN information reports

The Children and Families Act (Gov UK, 2014) provides a full account of what is expected to be included within a school's SEN Information Report. It is a document aimed at providing families with the information they need to understand how the school implements its SEND Policy. For this reason, it is important that it is easily located on the school website and readily accessible. It will be informed by, and aligned with, the expectations of provision set out in the Local Offer. Whilst the SEN Information Report is primarily for families, it can also be an effective tool to ensure that staff within the school have a common understanding of how the SEND Policy is implemented, for example the implementation of the graduated approach.

Figure 2.1 shows how the SEN Information Report, the Local Offer and the SEND Policy all fit together. Some schools prefer to have the SEND Policy and the SEN Information Report within the same document, but there is no requirement to do this. The SEND Policy is unlikely to change dramatically over time, whilst the SEN Information Report is more responsive and may change more frequently. The SEN Information Report should be reviewed annually and parents, pupils, the SENCO, the SEND Governor and other school leaders should be involved in this process.

The SEN Information Report is a governance responsibility and all school leaders should be involved in updating it. Whilst it might be the SENCO who writes the report in practice, it is governors who are responsible for assuring the quality of the content, that it is reviewed annually and that it is published on the school website. Governors should ensure that the SEN Information Report reflects its approach to all pupils with SEND, including those at the level of SEN support and those with EHC plans. Therefore, governors need to ensure they receive the draft SEN Information Report in advance so that they have sufficient time to scrutinise it before approving it for publication at a formal meeting of the board.

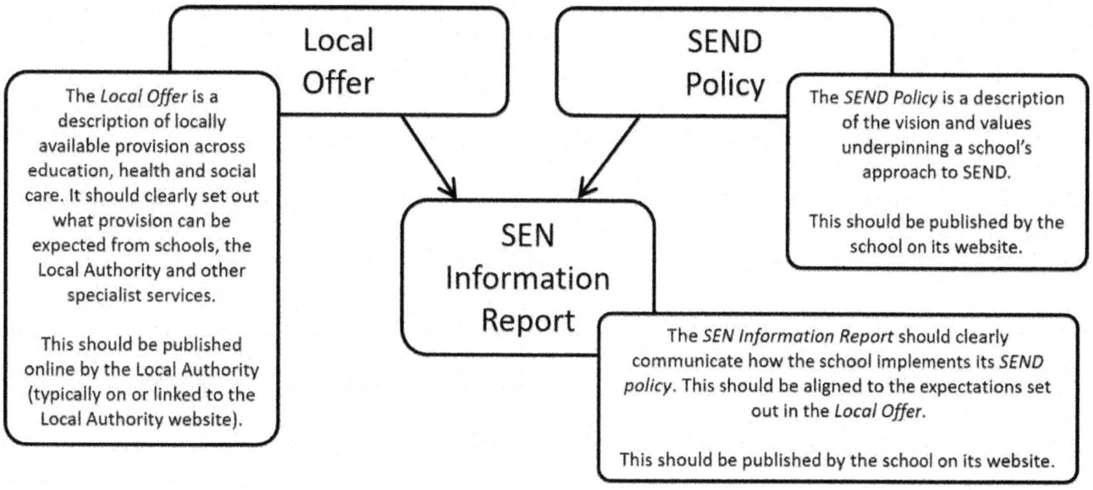

Figure 2.1 The SEN information report, the local offer and the SEND Policy.

> The SEND Code of Practice (DfE and DoH, 2015) includes the following list of items that <u>must</u> be included in a SEN Information Report:
>
> - The kinds of SEN that are provided for;
> - Policies for identifying children and young people with SEN and assessing their needs, including the name and contact details of the SENCO (mainstream schools);
> - Arrangements for consulting parents of children with SEN and involving them in their child's education;
> - Arrangements for consulting young people with SEN and involving them in their education;
> - Arrangements for assessing and reviewing children and young people's progress towards outcomes. This should include the opportunities available to work with parents and young people as part of this assessment and review;

- Arrangements for supporting children and young people in moving between phases of education and in preparing for adulthood. As young people prepare for adulthood, outcomes should reflect their ambitions, which could include higher education, employment, independent living and participation in society;
- The approach to teaching children and young people with SEN;
- How adaptations are made to the curriculum and the learning environment of children and young people with SEN;
- The expertise and training of staff to support children and young people with SEN, including how specialist expertise will be secured;
- Evaluating the effectiveness of the provision made for children and young people with SEN;
- How children and young people with SEN are enabled to engage in activities available with children and young people in the school who do not have SEN;
- Support for improving emotional and social development. This should include extra pastoral support arrangements for listening to the views of children and young people with SEN and measures to prevent bullying;
- How the school involves other bodies, including health and social care bodies, Local Authority support services and voluntary sector organisations, in meeting children and young people's SEN and supporting their families;
- Arrangements for handling complaints from parents of children with SEN about the provision made at the school.

The above requirements are a baseline expectation. SEN Information Reports that represent best practice go beyond these basic requirements and ensure the document is as accessible and impactful as possible. For example, in specifying how the school involves Local Authority support services, the obvious approach is to draw from the Local Offer from the school's home Local Authority when writing the SEN Information Report. However, many schools are likely to draw on multiple Local Offers. This can occur when a school is near to a Local Authority border, so it admits children from neighbouring authorities or it could be a special school with students attending from Local Authorities that are some distance away. It may be also the case that health services and education services use slightly different boundaries. The most effective SEN Information Reports provide information about other relevant Local Offers, as reflected in Figure 2.2.

Other features of best practice that governors may wish to include in their SEN Information Report are:

- **Indicate any changes:** Current pupils with SEND and their families should be familiar with the school's SEN Information Report. When the report goes through its annual review and update, they should not have to wade through the entire new document to identify the changes. Consider highlighting any changes or publishing a list of changes from the previous report as an appendix.
- **Review information:** The annual review date for the SEN Information Report should be clearly specified. In the spirit of coproduction, there should be a clear invitation for pupils and families to participate in this process and information should be provided as to how they can express their interest to get involved.

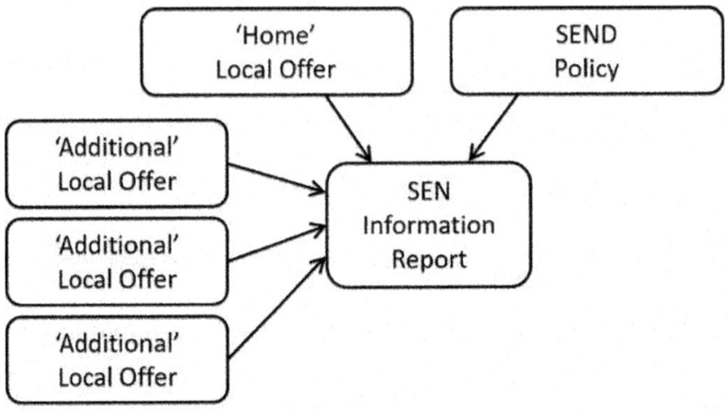

Figure 2.2 Drawing from multiple local offers.

- **Glossary of terms:** Education is a sector that is full of acronyms and sector-specific technical jargon. The context of SEND arguably adds to an already complicated set of educational language. Sometimes, this is unavoidable, but do consider including a glossary in the appendices as a useful reference point. Better still, hyperlink any glossary words in the online version of the SEN Information Report so that the definitions are more immediately accessible.
- **Assistive technology:** The availability of assistive technology can vary widely between schools. Specify what is available to encourage pupils and their families to request to use technology that will support them in accessing the curriculum. Providing examples of how the technology is currently used will also be useful here.
- **Access arrangements:** The processes in relation to access arrangements can be a source of worry for some pupils and their families. It is also an area that SENCOs receive a significant amount of correspondence about from families at certain times of the year. Including a list of frequently asked questions (and the school's responses!) may well save the SENCO significant time as well as manage expectations about what access arrangements may be available.
- **The graduated approach:** Whilst the four spiral-like stages of the graduated approach are often included in SEN Information Reports, it is useful to spell out how this is expected to be interpreted and implemented in the context of a specific school. Including some examples of how the approach has been used with previous pupils (anonymised) to refine provision and maximise impact will help both teachers and staff to develop a common understanding.
- **SEN funding:** Earlier in this chapter, emphasis was placed on the importance of identifying the value of the SEN notional budget, understanding how it has been spent and evaluating its impact. Whilst this information helps governors make strategic decisions, it can be presented in the SEN Information Report to be open and transparent with families about how the school uses its funding to support pupils with SEND. Some schools use the format of a costed provision map to present this information.
- **Current provision and practice:** Sometimes, the SEN Information Report can focus so much on specialist provision and how practice is developing to meet needs that the excellent practice already in place can be overlooked. Often, schools have already taken many steps to prevent pupils with SEND being treated less favourably than other pupils. It is good to share this with families so that they know what the school has already put into place and it will also help to ensure that schools do not inadvertently cease existing effective practice.
- **Individual contact information:** In addition to the name and contact details for the SENCO, it is useful to include the name and contact details for other relevant individuals. This could include the SEND Governor, an Assistant SENCO or key people within the Local Authority (subject to any data protection requirements of course!). Such individual details provide a more welcoming and encouraging feel than generic email addresses. Including telephone contact details if possible increases accessibility as not everybody has ready access to email or the internet and some people will be more comfortable discussing their questions or concerns than putting them in writing.

The accessibility of the SEN Information Report is an essential feature of its effectiveness. An excellent document packed with useful information that cannot be accessed by those who need it will be ineffective. The list below should be a useful sense-check in relation to some of the common accessibility barriers, but it is by no means exhaustive. Governors are strongly encouraged to consult with families about the accessibility of the document as a standard aspect of the review process that takes place each year.

- Once the document is on the website, ensure it is freely accessible and does not require a password to download or open it.
- Ensure the document is in a format that is accessible to those with sensory impairments, for example hearing impairments, vision impairments or multi-sensory impairments. In practical terms, there are file formats that are compatible with screen readers, overlays and other accessibility tools, but some make this very difficult. Guidance on accessible communication is readily available from multiple sources (e.g., DWP and ODI, 2018; RNIB, 2017; NHS England, 2017).
- Use plain English and short sentences, since SEN Information Reports can be lengthy documents. Consider whether some information is more effectively communicated using illustrations, graphs or flow diagrams. This will help to break up the document and avoid dense blocks of text.

- Have some printed copies of the report available at the school reception. Some people will find it easier to read a hard copy where they can highlight it and make notes. This will also help to address the issue of some families not having internet access or printing facilities.
- Make the online version of the document as interactive as possible. This could include hyperlinks to other key policies, websites and resources, such as the Local Offer, the SEND Policy and support organisations. The key policies discussed earlier in the chapter can be hyperlinked to, such as 'supporting pupils with medical conditions', the 'accessibility plan' and the 'behaviour principles written statement'. Links to relevant (short) videos will also help to make the document more accessible.
- If the school has any social media presence, then videos that have been specifically designed for the school could be used as a way into the SEN Information Report. For example, there could be a 30-second clip of a teacher briefly summarising the stages of the graduated approach, which encourages watchers to access the SEN Information Report to find out more and access the full details.

Ultimately the SEN Information Report should be a document that is both informative and celebratory. It allows the school to provide clarity about how they meet the needs of pupils with SEND and also to celebrate their successes in relation to SEND and inclusion.

Summary

This chapter has introduced the six key features of effective governance and explored them through the lens of SEND and inclusion. Having read this chapter, you should have now developed your knowledge and understanding of:

- The suggested responsibilities for board members in relation to SEND and inclusion, both individually and as a whole
- The leadership of SEND
- Assessing progress towards inclusion by considering stakeholder perceptions
- School policies that are particularly relevant for SEND and inclusion
- The Equality Act 2010
- The Children and Families Act 2014
- The SEN notional budget
- The Local Offer and the school's SEND Policy
- The SEN Information Report

The key ten messages that should be taken from this chapter are:

1. **All governors, trustees and school leaders should be familiar with Chapter 6 of the SEND Code of Practice (**DfE and DoH, 2015). This chapter is 20 pages long and it includes essential information in relation to SEND provision in schools. This could be incorporated into the induction process for new governors and trustees.
2. **Give SEND the same status as pupil premium.** Governors should ensure that SEND has an equivalent status to pupil premium at board meetings, including equivalent evaluations of the impact of targeted funding. Specific consideration should be given to the cohort of pupils that have SEND, but are also eligible for pupil premium.
3. **Ensure that all governors and trustees have access to specialist knowledge and information in relation to SEND and inclusion.** Providing access to professional communities of practice and information/support services is an important aspect of effective SEND governance, since it allows governors to more effectively hold school leaders to account. Such services could include membership of *nasen*, The Key or the National Governance Association.
4. **Every leader a leader of SEND.** It is important not to rely only on the SEND Governor to provide effective SEND governance – all board members have responsibility for SEND and inclusion. The SEND reforms established the principle that every teacher is a teacher of SEND, but in order for this to be realised, every leader needs to be a leader of SEND.

5. **Think SEND!** For every decision made by the board, consideration should be given to how that decision will impact pupils with SEND. Having SEND built-in to strategic decision-making will help to avoid unintended negative consequences.
6. **Coproduction is an essential feature of effective SEND governance.** Governors should ensure that appropriate mechanisms are in place for families to work in partnership with schools at all levels of decision-making.
7. **Governors should use data to inform strategic decision-making.** Governors should seek to triangulate evidence from multiple data sources to increase validity and ensure that decisions are as impactful as possible.
8. **Governors should have a common understanding of SEND and inclusion for the specific context of their school.** This chapter provided some key questions that can be used in board meetings to ensure that governors understand the profile of SEND in their school.
9. **Ethical leadership is a key feature of effective SEND governance.** It is important that board-level decisions are always made in the interests of pupils at the school. Governors and trustees should consider external factors (such as accountability and funding) as secondary priorities compared to doing the right thing.
10. **A high-quality SEN Information Report will support both school staff and families.** Investment in getting the SEN Information Report right will ensure it can be used by staff as a guide for the implementation of the school's SEND Policy. It should also answer many of the questions that pupils with SEND and their families may have in relation to SEND provision at the school.

Note

1 The word 'inclusive' may not be appropriate to use in a survey with younger children, so this question may need to be adapted for different groups. There is also a question about the extent to which 'inclusion' refers to SEND or to other areas, such as sexuality or ethnicity.

3 Reviewing SEND governance and SEND provision

Chapters 1 and 2 were focused on developing a better understanding of SEND and inclusion as well as how effective governance can improve SEND provision. Chapter 3 will consider in practical terms how boards can evaluate their current position in relation to the effectiveness of their SEND governance and the school's SEND provision. The role of governance action planning, SEND learning walks and effective questioning in board meetings will also be explored.

Governance action plan

It could be argued that effective governance is more about the journey than the destination. There is no silver bullet for achieving 'perfect governance' and if there was it is likely that the vast majority of boards would be excelling already. The reality is that a constant drive for continuous improvement can be the distinguishing factor between effective and ineffective school governance. Governing bodies that are determined to be successful will often have a governance action plan (or a governance improvement plan) in place. This is important because effective SEND governance is likely to be positively correlated with the overall effectiveness of governance.

The content of a governance action plan can be informed by data from a myriad of sources, including:

- Governor skills and knowledge audit
- External review of governance (could include peer review)
- Self-evaluation
- Data from SEND learning walks
- Best practice from governance in other schools/settings
- Feedback from key stakeholders (e.g., pupils, families, staff and volunteers)
- External feedback (e.g., from the Local Authority or the central team within a multi-academy trust [MAT])
- Published advice or guidance (e.g., from government or from professional bodies such as *nasen*, NASS or the NGA)
- Academic research (e.g., from universities, the Education Endowment Foundation or educational think tanks)
- The wider school improvement plan

Some governance action plans are a natural extension of the school improvement plan and therefore use the same template. This is a useful approach since it allows boards to be proactive in demonstrating how they are contributing to whole school priorities. Similarly, it means that priorities identified at board level can be reflected in the wider activity of the school.

A second possible approach is to structure the governance action plan around the six key features of effective governance introduced in Chapter 2: strategic leadership, accountability, people, structures, compliance and evaluation. In taking such an approach, governors should incorporate the principle of 'Think SEND!' introduced in Chapter 2. In practice, this could consist of an additional column to proactively consider the impact of each strand of work on pupils with SEND (or indeed protected characteristics more broadly). Table 3.1 shows what a completed governance action plan might look like at the end of the autumn term structured in this way. This example is based on annual targets and termly monitoring, but for more strategic developments, a multi-year plan with annual review may be more appropriate.

Table 3.1 Example of a completed governance action plan.

Governance action plan			*Last reviewed: Jan 2021 Next review due: May 2021*					*Termly progress update and next steps*		
Key areas of effective governance	*Ref*	*Area for development*	*Proposed actions*	*Think SEND!*	*Led by who?*	*By when?*	*RAG*	*Autumn*	*Spring*	*Summer*
Strategic leadership (setting direction; culture, values and ethos; decision-making; collaborative working with stakeholders and partners; risk management)	1.1	Ensuring the school retains its inclusive ethos	Governors make appropriate resources available to ensure effective provision for key groups, including **SEND**, **pupil premium** and **most able**.	Need to ensure a 'balance of inclusion' since what is inclusive for one group of pupils with SEND may not be inclusive for another.	Resources Committee	Jan-21		Pupil Premium impact validated by LA visit and discussed at full board. Headteacher says there is no SEN notional budget? Need to investigate further with LA.		
	1.2	Possible academisation	The option of academisation is reviewed annually by governors with any changes to the current position clearly communicated to key stakeholders, including parents and staff.	Consider the inclusivity and values-base of any MAT we may join. Could a MAT provide greater access to specialist provision (e.g., via special schools within the MAT)? Ensure academisation costs do not reduce funding available (e.g., SEN notional budget).	Chair	Apr-21		N/A - Works has not yet begun on this strand. To be reviewed in Spring.		
	1.3	Stakeholder engagement	Governors to review the cycle of questionnaires (staff, parent and pupil) to assess impact on provision and outcomes. The process should be made more streamlined wherever possible.	An opportunity to check our coproduction is meaningful and effective. Triangulate views of SEND and inclusion.	Parent Governors	Nov-20		Coproduction and SEND provision rated highly by staff and pupils, but less favourably by parents. Explore with the Parent Council?		

Accountability (educational improvement, rigorous analysis of data, financial frameworks and accountability, financial management and monitoring, staffing and performance management, external accountability)	2.1	Monitoring of reading as a key area for educational improvement	Evidence shows that SLT initiatives to improve reading are effective, including an improvement in reading progress and attainment at key stage 1 and 2 statutory assessments and evidence of an increase in children's love for reading.	Is the board confident that SLT initiatives are sufficiently differentiated for children with developmental delay or literacy difficulties?	Quality of education committee	Jul-21	Internal data shows attainment levels of reading increasing gradually. Parental reading task force up and running. Staff CPD included a focus on dyslexia. Work on track.
	2.2	Journey to outstanding (are we Ofsted ready? How do we know?)	Governors and SLT to benchmark against the provision in other similar outstanding schools. All governors and SLT to have a clear and common understanding of what outstanding looks like and what we need to do to get there.	The Ofsted framework means that no school can be graded outstanding unless they can also demonstrate that they are inclusive. Where are our inclusion gaps?	All	Dec-20	Visits to other similar outstanding schools have happened. Not deemed very useful as context-specific. Board and SLT know inclusion strengths, but are struggling to identify gaps. External input needed?
	2.3	Governor's knowledge of school data and school priorities	All governors to be familiar with school data, and regional and national data sets and confident in asking probing questions and identifying trends and areas of under/over performance.	Ensure data is broken down against SEND and (if appropriate) the four broad areas of need. Look at SEND-specific data sets to benchmark the school against other schools.	All	Dec-20	The Headteacher has provided the breakdown asked for and the SENCO has presented twice to the board. Social, emotional and mental health is a group with worse outcomes than for pupils with SEND in general at school. Need to understand more about this and what we are doing.

(*Continued*)

Table 3.1 Example of a completed governance action plan. (*Continued*)

Governance action plan			*Last reviewed: Jan 2021 Next review due: May 2021*					*Termly progress update and next steps*		
Key areas of effective governance	*Ref*	*Area for development*	*Proposed actions*	*Think SEND!*	*Led by who?*	*By when?*	*RAG*	*Autumn*	*Spring*	*Summer*
	2.4	HLP children	Governors to seek evidence from school leaders about the support, development and achievement of learners with HLP.	Within this cohort of children, some will have DME. Ensure evidence looks at both how needs are meet as well as academic/other outcomes.	SEND Gov	Nov-20		Termly meeting of SENCO and SEND governor showed that responsibility for HLP was not joined up with SEND/inclusion, so pupils with DME not identified. SENCO and Gifted and Talented Coordinator now working together. Monitor.		
People (building an effective team)	3.1	New governor induction and development	Governors to review the induction programme for new governors, including in-school provision, LA training and peer mentoring systems. Development of a governor induction pack tailored from resources from The Key and NGA.	Ensure that SEND and inclusion play a central role in induction. What is the basic level of knowledge we expect all governors to have? Aside from the SEND Governor, who else is/should be accessing SEND training.	Clerk	Dec-20		SEND content is included as part of induction, but it is out-of-date and needs to be revised. SEND governor and SENCO to progress this with clerk.		
	3.2	Advanced clerking (additional training, checking of statutory requirements, policies overview, etc.)	Governors to consider whether we are making the most of the clerk. Where necessary provide advanced training and development to allow the clerk to undertake additional duties, e.g., policy maintenance, review of statutory online information, etc.	Worth looking at how the SEN Information Report has changed over time. Does it reflect the SEND Policy? How is SEND and inclusion reflected across all of our statutory policies?	Vice-chair and clerk	Dec-20		Clerk is happy to do further training to be able to offer more to their school. Budget limitations since clerk is paid by the hour, not as volunteer. Explore with Finance Committee. Clerk is exploring alignment between SEND policy and SEN Information Report.		

Structures (roles and responsibilities)	4.1	Strengthen succession planning for key functions (Chair, Vice Chairs, SEND, safeguarding, finance, GDPR)	Link governance roles (including shadow roles) are working effectively. There is a need to ensure there is a 'governor-in-waiting' for all key roles. Where possible these roles should be handed over before the incumbent stands down to ensure a smooth transition.	Should we consider having an Assistant SEND Governor? Should this role rotate after a fixed period of say two years?	Chair	Jun-21	Limited succession planning in place for most roles. Significant work to do in this area. Governor skills audit suggests we have what we need within the board, but there may be an issue of workload/time. Consider use of Associate Board Members.
Compliance (statutory and contractual requirements)	5.1	Policies overview	Development of a policy overview document that can be used to monitor the status of all policies and to plan for the cycle of renewals.	Include a SEND column in the overview to summarise the impact of each policy on pupils with SEND.	Clerk	Apr-21	N/A – Work has not yet begun on this strand. To be reviewed in Spring.
Evaluation (managing self-review and personal skills; managing and developing the board's effectiveness)	6.1	Peer review of governance	Consider the mutual benefits of a peer review process with another board locally to share best practice.	Ensure that a SEND Governance Review feeds into this broader process.	Chair	Jul-21	SEND Governance Review has taken place using a local consultant. Peer review book in January 2021.
	6.2	Maintain governor evaluation process	Ensure that the current appraisal system for governors is engaged with by all governors and that it genuinely impacts on improving governance.	As part of the end of cycle appraisal discussion, could governors reflect on the impact of governance on pupils with SEND?	Chair	Jul-21	N/A – Work has not yet begun on this strand. To be reviewed in Spring.

Reviewing SEND governance

As indicated above, a review of SEND governance should be one of the key elements feeding into a governance action plan. There may be several other reasons why schools choose to conduct a SEND governance review, including:

- SEND is flagged by Ofsted as an area for development.
- The school has a disproportionate number (high or low) of pupils with SEND compared to regional and national averages.
- The school has identified a higher than average complexity in relation to the overall profile of needs.
- Outcomes (academic and/or otherwise) for pupils with SEND are below expectations.
- Pupils or their parents/carers are dissatisfied with SEND provision at the school.
- Improving inclusion is a priority in the school development plan.

In considering a review of SEND governance, a good starting point would perhaps be the *SEND Governance Review Guide* (Rossiter, 2020), part of a suite of resources published via the Whole School SEND consortium. This suite of resources is free and can be downloaded from the SEND Gateway (www.sendgateway.org.uk). At the heart of the suite is the *SEND Review Guide* (Bartram and Patel, 2020), which facilitates a school-led approach to improving inclusive provision. This is supported by a series of other guides and supporting resources designed to span all elements of SEND within a school or a trust. All of the guides within the suite are available in an editable, white label format so they can be tailored to match the needs of an individual school. Before exploring the *SEND Governance Review Guide* (Rossiter, 2020) in more detail, a summary of the Whole School SEND suite of resources is given in Table 3.2.

Table 3.2 Summary of Whole School SEND resources.

Who is it for?	*What is the resource called?*	*What is it for?*
Headteachers, Executive Headteachers and trustees	MAT SEND Review Guide (Reeve, 2020)*	A framework to support external, peer or self-review in relation to effective SEND governance and provision across a group of schools, for example a MAT, a federation or indeed any group of schools working within a common structure. The review is structured around five key areas: • Leadership • Identification • Tracking and monitoring • Intervention • Provision
Parents/carers	A guide to making conversations count for all families (Knight and Busk, 2020)*	Under the banner of 'Ask Listen Do', this leaflet provides a list of questions that families may wish to ask those who support their children at school. The aim is to support families and schools to work together through honest and open dialogue.
Governors in all schools	*SEND Governance Review Guide* (Rossiter, 2020)*	A framework to support external, peer or self-review in relation to effective SEND governance. The review is structured around five key areas: • Strategic leadership • Accountability • Structures and processes • People management • Evaluation
Headteachers	Effective SENCO Deployment (Moloney, 2020)*	A tool to assist school leaders to identify how their SENCO might be deployed more effectively. The tool is structured around five key themes: • Membership of the senior leadership team • The team around the SENCO • Effective performance management • Time • Effective coproduction with parents

Who is it for?	*What is the resource called?*	*What is it for?*
	Demonstrating Inclusion Tool (Chamberlain, 2020)*	Under the banner of 'Every Leader is a Leader of SEND', this tool is designed to empower leaders to reflect on and improve their inclusion of pupils with SEND. The tool is structured around five key areas: • Inclusive leadership • Inclusive teaching and learning • Drawing on expertise to enrich school experience • Deployment of resources in an evidence-informed way • Pupil achievements and outcomes
SENCOs and other senior leaders	SEND Review Guide (Bartram and Patel, 2020)*	A framework to support external, peer or self-review in relation to effective SEND provision. The review is structured around eight key areas: • Outcomes for pupils with SEND • Leadership of SEND • The quality of teaching and learning for pupils with SEND • Working with pupils and parents/carers of pupils with SEND • Assessment and identification • Monitoring, tracking and evaluation • The efficient use of resources • The quality of SEND provision
	SENCO Induction Pack (Wharton et al, 2019)*	A reference tool to support SENCOs with the key operational requirements of the role from day one. It includes: • The role of the SENCO • Legislation and guidance • Identifying and understanding areas of need • Using the graduated approach and SEN support • The SENCO's role in EHC plans • Monitoring and managing provision • Working with children and young people • Working in partnership with parents, carers and others • Working with support staff • The role of the SENCO in leading professional development • SENCO and practitioner wellbeing • The SENCO, self-evaluation and Ofsted • The role of the SENCO in organising access arrangements
	TA Deployment Review Guide (Webster, 2020)*	A framework to support external, peer or self-review in relation to the deployment and management of teaching assistants. The review is structured around eight key areas: • Leadership of TAs • Strategic use of TAs • Classroom deployment • Effective interactions • Preparation and training • Structured interventions • Monitoring, tracking and evaluation • Outcomes or improving outcomes
	Preparing for Adulthood from the Earliest Years Review Guide (Stobbs et al, 2018)*	A framework to support external, peer or self-review in relation to how schools prepare pupils for adulthood. The review is structured around eight key areas: • Leadership • Outcomes • Curriculum and personalisation • Quality of teaching and learning • Working with pupils with SEND and their parents and carers • Assessment and identification • Monitoring and evaluation • Efficient use of resources

(Continued)

Table 3.2 Summary of Whole School SEND resources. (*Continued*)

Who is it for?	*What is the resource called?*	*What is it for?*
Individuals in schools or settings	SEND Reflection Framework (Knight, 2020)*	A tool to support teachers to evaluate the extent to which they can meet the requirements of pupils with SEND. The tool is structured around sets of statements in seven key areas: • Knowledge of the learner • Quality of teaching and learning • Creating an environment conducive of effective learning • Transitions and change • Systems and processes • Working and communicating with families • Working with other professionals and the wider community
	Early Years SEND Review Guide (Early Years SEND Partnership, 2019)*	A framework to support external, peer or self-review in relation to effective SEND provision in an early years setting. The review is structured around six key areas: • Leadership of SEND • Outcomes and the quality of teaching and learning for children with SEND • Working with children and parents/carers of children with SEND • Assessment and identification • The efficient use of resources • The quality of SEND provision
	Condition-Specific Introductory Videos for NQTs (Whole School SEND, 2020)*	A series of videos aimed at developing newly qualified teachers' knowledge of SEND and introducing helpful resources and tips for the classroom. The specific conditions covered include: • Acquired brain injury • ADHD • Autism • Down's syndrome • Dyscalculia • Dyslexia • Dyspraxia • Social, emotional and mental health • Hearing impairment • Speech, language and communication • Physical disability • Vision impairment

* These resources often had a large number of authors/contributors, who are typically listed in full within each of the documents themselves. For the purposes of referencing, the original lead authors only have been included here.

Note: Some of the resources were republished with minimal changes (for example updated terminology) in 2020, but have been around for several years.

Thinking specifically about the *SEND Governance Review Guide* (Rossiter, 2020), each of the five sections has a list of suggested themes and areas to explore. These themes are set out as a series of statements grouped by what the school/setting demonstrates and what the board demonstrates. The *MAT SEND Review Guide* (Reeve, 2020) takes a more holistic approach with the governance elements built into the overall sets of statements.

All of the review guides are intended to be used as a framework for critical reflection and strategic planning rather than as a simple checklist of compliance. The intention is that they facilitate structured discussions, which ultimately result in improved SEND provision and therefore improved outcomes for pupils with SEND.

The way in which the review guides are used varies depending upon the specific context in which they are being applied. Self, peer and external review are three possible approaches and Table 3.3 explores the relative merits of each approach in relation to cost, time, reputational risk, reliability and validity, data protection, leadership prioritisation and specialist expertise. It should be made clear here that each approach to review has merit and that these merits will vary by school. The table is a useful starting point for considering which approaches to take, but this should always be considered in the context of your own particular circumstances.

Table 3.3 Relative merits of self, peer and external review.

		Self-review		*Peer review*		*External review*
Cost	✓	Low cost if using existing staffing to lead a review.	✓	Keep costs low by two schools agreeing to review each other as a contra arrangement.		If consultancy is required, an average-sized school might expect to pay between £1k and £2k for a review.
Time	✓	This will take time, but it is generally less time consuming than either peer or external evaluation, both of which will also require internal staff time (e.g., collating documents, arranging meetings, etc.).		In addition to involvement in your own review, you may need to be involved in reviewing for another school, which will be a significant time commitment.	✓	Engaging an external reviewer can save time if an experienced reviewer is appointed. However, time will still be needed to conduct a self-evaluation and to support the review process.
Reputational risk	✓	Any issues identified can remain internal to the school.	✓	Assuming the peer conducting the review is a trusted colleague, they will be supportive, rather than unnecessarily critical, where issues are identified.		Confidentiality is a key aspect of external review, but nevertheless, this approach carries the greatest risk in relation to external individuals having detailed knowledge of issues.
Reliability and validity		Unintentionally, there may be unconscious bias. Identifying your own areas for development is important, but also fraught with difficulty.		Unintentionally, peers may 'sugar coat' issues so that the professional relationship is not damaged.	✓	An experienced reviewer can moderate judgements against what they have seen in other schools. They are independent enough to be more objective and can call out issues with less individual risk.
Data protection	✓	All data remain within the school.		Data has to be shared with the peer reviewer. Whilst confidential/anonymised, this may be insufficient for a peer reviewer with existing knowledge of the school community.		Data has to be shared with an external consultant. Measures to protect data and ensure it is deleted post-review are important.
Leadership prioritisation		It may be easier for a leader who disagrees with the conclusions or recommendations of an internal review to dismiss it or not take the necessary action.	✓	Peer pressure could be a useful mechanism to ensure any recommendations are taken seriously by school leaders.	✓	An external reviewer can insist that conclusions and recommendations are shared with leaders and board members and push for a follow-up visit, both of which will help to prioritise actions.
Specialist expertise		The school is limited by the specialist expertise within its workforce.		The quality of peer relationships may be a limiting factor with this approach.	✓	The school can identify a reviewer with the required level of experience and expertise.

Note – The ticks in the table indicate whether the particular review approach is likely to be appropriate in the context of specific parameters. However, this is simply a starting point since every school and situation will be unique.

A common approach is to use the review guides to undertake a self-evaluation and then have this validated, challenged and discussed through a process of peer or external review. The *SEND Review Guide* (Bartram and Patel, 2020) advocates a six-stage process:

1. **Identification:** Request for a review is made
2. **Self-evaluation:** School completes self-evaluation of current provision
3. **Preparation:** The reviewer requests preparatory information, analyses relevant data and confirms programme
4. **School visit:** The reviewer visits the school, collects evidence and delivers verbal feedback
5. **Reporting:** The reviewer submits a written report within a timescale agreed with the school
6. **Follow-up:** The school may agree follow-up visits and support

In relation to identifying a suitable individual for conducting the peer or external review, it is important to ensure that they have the necessary experience and expertise. Organisations like *nasen*, who host Whole School SEND, can help to identify reviewers. Similarly, National Leaders of Education, Specialist Leaders of Education and National Leaders of Governance are a useful pool of professionals to draw from.

From a board perspective, there are two overarching themes in relation to SEND reviews. The first is in relation to SEND provision and the second is in relation to SEND governance. Therefore, if there is sufficient capacity and resource available, it makes sense to conduct a range of different SEND reviews simultaneously to gain multiple insights into these two areas. This will allow for a more holistic analysis of SEND provision and SEND governance, so that any resulting action plan can be as impactful as possible.

Lastly, there are some alternatives to SEND reviews that are worth noting. In particular, the *Inclusion Quality Mark* (McCann and McCann, 2004) is a well-respected and long-established accreditation, which follows a similar approach of self-evaluation followed by a validation visit from an external professional. The Inclusion Quality Mark takes a broad view of inclusion, the scope of which spans SEND, HLP and DME amongst other areas.

Whilst SEND reviews can be insightful and useful, they are also resource-intensive. It is up to a school how often they conduct SEND reviews, but my own experience suggests that a relatively small number of schools conduct them annually and that it is more typical for them to be conducted once every few years or as a one-off in response to SEND being identified as a school-improvement priority (e.g., by Ofsted, the MAT or the Local Authority).

SEND learning walks

In addition to strategic SEND reviews, it is important for governors to have other systems and processes in place that allow them to monitor the quality of SEND provision more regularly. One such process is a *SEND learning walk*, which can be completed in just a few hours. In general, a learning walk consists of a series of structured classroom visits by senior teachers and other colleagues (Skretta, 2007). An effective learning walk goes beyond a basic checklist and should instead seek to draw out insightful observations that can then inform purposeful professional discussion (Finch, 2010).

The concept of a SEND learning walk being introduced here has an obvious focus on SEND and inclusion, but also seeks to extend the traditional learning walk in three distinct ways.

1. Unlike traditional learning walks, which are generally about school leaders gaining insights into pupils' learning, SEND learning walks are essentially a familiarisation process focused on helping governors to learn more about SEND provision. It could be thought of as a method of gaining contextual evidence to enhance the reports received in the boardroom.
2. SEND learning walks are governor-led, which builds on the concept of every leader being a leader of SEND that was introduced earlier. It is wholly appropriate for governors to conduct learning walks as a method of gathering first-hand insights of SEND provision, but it is important that governors also remember they are not there to make judgements on the quality of teaching and learning. Indeed, learning walks are not generally intended to be used for measuring the performance of individual professionals (Baker and King, 2013). School leaders and other key members of staff will generally accompany governors.

3. SEND learning walks go beyond classroom visits by bringing in other forms of evidence around the theme of SEND and inclusion, so that triangulation can occur (Robson, 2002, pp 174–175). This structured approach strengthens one of the fundamental principles of learning walks, which is to facilitate deeper and more intimate connections between strategic leaders and day-to-day provision (Lemons and Helsing, 2009).

The evidence gathered from one or more SEND learning walks can feed directly into an action plan or into any of the SEND reviews being conducted at a more strategic level. Critics of governor involvement in learning walks could make the case that they are too operational. However, for governors to be effective with strategic decision-making, they will sometimes need to test the operational (Killey, 2018).

There is no universally agreed format for a SEND learning walk, but one possible approach is described below, which can be used as a framework for conducting a SEND learning walk in your own school. This model is led by the SEND Governor, but it actively involves all governors (or as many as possible). Governors convene before the start of the school day, where the SEND Governor provides a briefing on how the morning will work and allocates the key roles and responsibilities. Governors then spend up to 2 hours working on activities in pairs or small groups before reconvening. Some of these activities will be more about shadowing a process led by a member of staff to preserve clarity between the strategic leadership role of governors and the strategic and operational leadership role of Headteachers. The specific activities will vary depending on the specific circumstances, but they would typically include:

- Discussion with the Headteacher and SENCO in relation to the school's self-evaluation of SEND provision.
- Focus groups with families to understand their perspectives on the effectiveness of SEND provision. It is important to ensure a broad range of families are involved to span the complexity and different types of need.
- Focus groups with children to hear their views about SEND and inclusion at school.
- Lesson visits with a senior member of staff (including visits to individual and small group interventions) to:
    - witness SEND provision first-hand;
    - get a sense of how support staff are being deployed;
    - see examples of inclusiveness in classroom environments.
- Shadowing senior members of staff undertaking a book scrutiny with a focus on whether there is a consistency of high aspirations for all pupils, including those with SEND.
- Data scrutiny for all relevant data sets, which may include staff surveys, pupil surveys, family surveys, progress data, attendance data, exclusion rates, etc.

Each group should seek to identify two key strengths and one key recommendation for an area of development before reconvening as a full group with the full board of governors as well as both the Headteacher and the SENCO. Each group should share their findings and care should be taken to use triangulation (Robson, 2002, pp 174–175) to identify common strengths and recommendations. On the basis of this, priorities can be agreed, which can directly inform an action plan.

This model for conducting a SEND learning walk provides governors with direct insights into SEND provision to inform strategic decision-making. However, it also has other advantages, such as helping to develop governors' knowledge and reinforcing the principle that all governors have responsibility for SEND, not just the SEND Governor.

Discussing SEND provision in board meetings

SEND should be an area that is regularly discussed by governors. As well as being reactive in responding to any data and information that is presented, governors should be proactive in asking questions about SEND and inclusion. Table 3.4 includes a list of some questions that governors may wish to ask along with possible follow-up questions if they are not covered as part of the school's responses. This is not an exhaustive list, and some of the questions have different levels of relevance depending on whether the school is a special school or a mainstream school. One approach might be to consider one or two questions at each meeting to ensure coverage of the key questions over a period of time.

Table 3.4 SEND questions for governors to ask in board meetings.

Governor questions	*Follow-up questions*
What is our school's profile of needs?	• What proportion of pupils has an EHC plan? • What proportion of pupils is at the level of SEN support? • What is the balance of pupils' primary needs in relation to the four broad areas of need? • How do these proportions compare with regional and national averages? • How has the school's profile of need changed over time? • Does the school's profile of need and trend data suggest that we are becoming more inclusive over time? • Is the school's approach to the identification of SEND accurate and consistent? How do we know?
Is coproduction effective?	• Are families equal and meaningful partners in determining SEND provision? • How does the school ensure that meetings, resources and information are accessible to families to support the overall aim of coproduction? • How often do parents/carers routinely discuss SEND provision with class teachers? • For pupils with EHC plans, what do families think about the effectiveness of the annual review process? • What changes has the school implemented over the past three years to improve coproduction?
What is the school's approach to SEND provision?	• To what extent is school's approach child-centred? • How are support staff deployed? For example, what is the balance between 1:1 support in classes, small group support, classroom support and interventions? • Do all teachers demonstrate that pupils with SEND in their classes are their responsibility? Or is SEND seen as a more specialist area that is primarily the responsibility of support staff or the SENCO? • How does quality-first teaching support pupils at the level of SEN support? • How does the school's approach to SEND provision differ from other local schools?
How does the school ensure that staff are well-prepared to meet the needs of pupils with SEND?	• Has the SENCO completed the National Award for SEN Coordination qualification? (NB – this is a Masters level qualification, which must be completed within three years of becoming a SENCO). • How often do staff receive training on SEND? What has been covered in recent training and what is coming up? • How is the SEN notional budget spent? What is its impact? • What external support does the school access (e.g., from the Local Authority or from specialist support services)? • Is the SENCO a member of *nasen*? Are classroom teachers and other staff members of *nasen*? Are the resources routinely accessed and used effectively? • Do staff feel confident about meeting the needs of pupils with SEND? What plans are in place to address any concerns? • Does the SENCO have sufficient time to carry out his/her role effectively?
How do the rates of progress, attainment, attendance and exclusions for pupils with SEND compare to those without SEND?	• Do pupils with SEND attend school as regularly as pupils without SEND? Are there any differences in attendance rates when data is analysed against the four broad areas of need? • To what extent have medical needs or social care needs impacted on attendance data? • What is the typical role of families in improving attendance or preventing exclusions? • Are pupils with SEND more likely to be excluded than pupils without SEND in this school? How does the school ensure that such exclusions are not a direct consequence of the school failing to meet pupils' needs? • Has any pupil been off-rolled? • For pupils with SEND that is not related to cognition and learning, how do rates of progress and attainment compare with pupils without SEND and with national averages?

Governor questions	*Follow-up questions*
What are the school's key priorities for improving SEND and inclusion?	• Is there a SEND action plan? Is this reflected in the main school improvement priorities? • Is there a common understanding of how to improve SEND and inclusion? • What action can governors take at a strategic level to support the school's implementation of improvements in SEND provision? • How are the key priorities embedded within the roles of all staff to ensure that responsibility extends beyond the SENCO? • What is the role of the SEND Governor in monitoring the school's progress in relation to the identified priorities? • Are families aware of the school's priorities for SEND and inclusion? Do they agree with them? What role did they have in shaping them?

Ongoing professional support

In addition to the formal structured methods of reviewing SEND governance and SEND provision outlined in this chapter, it can add significant value if governors take an active interest in SEND and inclusion more broadly. Having a governing body that champions inclusion and feels confident to discuss SEND at meetings will establish and sustain its strategic importance.

Governors should ensure they are engaging with organisations that will keep them updated on changing legislation, the latest research and emerging effective practice. The *National Governance Association* and *The Key* both have useful sets of resources for governors to draw from. At the more specialist end, organisations like *nasen* and *NASS* are excellent too (see Appendix 1).

Governors may wish to read around the subject – the *nasen Spotlight* series published by Routledge has a broad range of books, including this one (www.routledge.com/nasen-spotlight/book-series/FULNASEN)! Social media can also be a useful tool for understanding the different perspectives on issues and participating in the debate. Both LinkedIn and Facebook have a number of specialist groups that governors can join (including some international groups) and on Twitter, there are many key influencers to follow. Again, this is not an exhaustive list and not all are relevant for every context, but here are some useful social media starting points for SEND governance.

Table 3.5 Social media starting points for SEND governance.

Facebook	*Twitter*	*LinkedIn*
• SEN School Governors Forum https://www.facebook.com/groups/275750029669382/ • Jane – School Governor's Group https://www.facebook.com/groups/157908974411819/ • School Governors UK https://www.facebook.com/groups/821981841151894/ • Primary School Governors https://www.facebook.com/groups/421122718267705/ • School Governance Forum UK – Hub4Leaders https://www.facebook.com/groups/1694615894173366/ • *nasen* https://www.facebook.com/nasen.org/	@nasen_org @WholeSchoolSEND @NASSCHOOLS @SpecialSchVoice @prusaporguk @sencochat @NGAMedia @TheKeySL @SchoolsWeek @tes @RoutledgeEd @adamboddison @APPG_SEND @GovernorSchool @schoolgovernor @WirralGov @educationgovuk @TheCFEY @axcis @GL_Education @NisaiLearning	• Special Education Needs https://www.linkedin.com/groups/1838346/ • *nasen* https://www.linkedin.com/company/3851285/ • Making Special Education Work https://www.linkedin.com/groups/2812035/ • Special Needs Jungle https://www.linkedin.com/groups/4861198/ • School Governor https://www.linkedin.com/groups/3179873/ • School Governors in the UK https://www.linkedin.com/groups/160298/ • School Governance Network https://www.linkedin.com/groups/12149906/

Note – The above list does not include any organisations that focus on specific types of need, but there are many of those too across all three social media platforms.

Summary

This chapter was focused on the specific practicalities of reviewing SEND governance and SEND provision. Having read this chapter, you should now have developed your knowledge and understanding of:

- How to create a (SEND) governance action plan, including the range of potential sources that could be used to inform it.
- The suite of resources and guides available from Whole School SEND and how they fit together.
- The different approaches to reviewing SEND and governance that can be taken.
- What a SEND learning walk is and how to conduct one in your own school.
- Questions that can be asked at board meetings to facilitate professional discussions about SEND and inclusion.
- The ongoing professional support available in relation to SEND, governance and education more broadly.
- Where social media can inform and support SEND governance.

The ten key messages that should be taken from this chapter are:

1. **Effective governance is more about the journey than the destination.** Every board will have areas it needs to develop and there is no expectation of perfection. However, effective governance requires a constant drive for continuous improvement.
2. **Effective governance is directly related to effective SEND governance.** The fundamental principles of effective governance are as important to SEND governance as any specialist knowledge. Boards should take the opportunity to reflect regularly on the overall quality of their governance.
3. **A review of SEND governance can provide essential intelligence to inform a governance action plan.** When SEND governance is reviewed, it may expose strengths and areas for development in relation to governance more broadly. These insights should be captured and acted upon.
4. **The Whole School SEND suite of review guides are frameworks for critical reflection and strategic planning, not a simple checklist of compliance.** Every school is distinctive because their school community is unique and each school's journey is different. The review guides will help to ask the right questions, but the answers will not be the same for every school.
5. **Effective reviews of SEND provision and SEND governance draw on elements of self-evaluation, peer review and external review.** Schools may have practical limitations that determine their approach to reviewing, but where possible they should adopt a multi-faceted approach to maximise the potential impact.
6. **Learning walks can be a catalyst for purposeful professional discussion in the board room.** If implemented effectively, learning walks can facilitate deeper and more intimate connections between governors and those responsible for the operational running of the school.
7. **SEND learning walks reinforce the principle that SEND is the responsibility of all governors.** Governors have a corporate responsibility for SEND and care should be taken to ensure that this responsibility is not left to the SEND Governor alone.
8. **SEND learning walks can develop governors' knowledge of SEND.** First-hand insights into the school's SEND provision are likely to increase governors' confidence and competence in making associated decisions at board meetings.
9. **Governors should be both proactive and reactive when asking questions about SEND.** Boards can sometimes be better at asking questions in response to information presented to them than they are at asking targeted questions about areas of strategic importance. For SEND governance, both are essential.
10. **Governors should ensure they have access to ongoing professional support in relation to SEND governance.** When conducting a skills audit, asking about individuals' professional memberships will help to ensure the board has access to an appropriate range of external expertise and professional support.

4 The SENCO, the Headteacher and the SEND Governor

The aim of this chapter is to explore in more depth the role of the SENCO, the SEND Governor and the Headteacher, and how they work in harmony as a triangle of SEND leadership, as shown in Figure 4.1. By developing their understanding of the expectations of these three important roles, governors will be better placed to ensure they have an effective approach to support and challenge in the context of SEND and inclusion.

There will be a particular emphasis on the core responsibilities of the SENCO, since this knowledge will prove invaluable for the SEND Governor to carry out his/her own role successfully. This will lead onto a discussion of the practicalities of the SEND Governor's role describing what actions they need to take, as well as how, when and why.

Chapter 6 of the SEND Code of Practice (DfE and DoH, 2015) summarises the following basic expectations of the SEND leadership infrastructure in schools:

- Mainstream schools and academies must appoint a qualified teacher to be the named SENCO (p 92, p 108)
- Special schools, pupil referral units and some other types of settings are not required to appoint a named SENCO (p 92)
- Each school should appoint a SEND Governor to oversee the school's arrangements for SEND (p 92)
- Headteachers should use their SEND resources and expertise to support school improvement and to 'build the quality of whole-school provision' (p 92)
- Newly appointed SENCOs should complete the Masters level National Award in SEN Coordination qualification within three years of being appointed (p 108)
- The SENCO has a strategic role in relation to SEND and 'will be most effective if they are part of the school leadership team' (p 108)

There is sometimes debate about whether schools can share a SENCO, and the SEND Code of Practice (DfE and DoH, 2015, p 109) does provide some guidance on this, albeit open to multiple interpretations. Essentially, it says that smaller schools could share a SENCO if it is 'appropriate' and if they have sufficient time, resources and support to 'fulfil the role effectively'. The amount

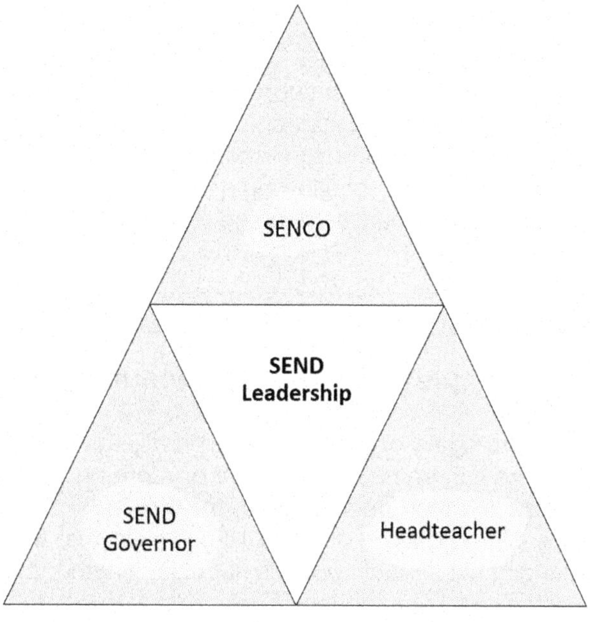

Figure 4.1 Triangle of SEND leadership.

of time that SENCOs need to undertake their role effectively is discussed in more detail later in this chapter. The code goes on to say that if there is evidence that a shared approach is not working, then it should not continue.

Three areas in which schools may have different interpretations of the guidance in relation to having a named SENCO are explained in this chapter. It should be noted that this book is not seeking to advocate any particular approach, but rather to discuss the relative merits and challenges of the different interpretations.

Example 1: Part-time SENCOs

A common approach in mainstream schools is for a teacher to have a proportion of their time protected to undertake the SENCO role. The amount of protected time varies between schools and depends on several factors such as the number of pupils (with SEND and overall), the availability of resources and the profile and complexity of needs.

Consider the scenario where a teacher has been allocated two days per week of protected time to undertake the SENCO role. The nature of school timetabling means that this is likely to be a regular time slot each week, but this can create logistical issues for the SENCO. They may need to attend meetings with external professionals (e.g., speech and language therapists, paediatric occupational therapists or educational psychologists) and these may not fall within the allocated two days of SENCO time. Meetings with families, lesson observations and external professional development are also examples of routine tasks that may not fall neatly within the allocated time.

Some schools tackle this by taking a more flexible approach to allocated time for SENCOs, but the nature of secondary school subject timetabling in particular means this is often not practical or can have an adverse impact on regular teaching groups.

If the available resources allow it, an alternative approach is to have a full-time SENCO, which will mitigate some of the issues discussed above. However, this is often not affordable for many schools. Another option used by some schools is to employ somebody part-time specifically to undertake the SENCO on the basis that they can be called upon as required. This is a scenario that can sometimes lead to schools sharing a SENCO, despite them not necessarily being 'smaller' schools as indicated in the SEND Code of Practice (DfE and DoH, 2015).

The sharing in this context could be a SENCO undertaking the role in two separate schools, but with each school having a separate contract of employment with the SENCO. From the perspective of each individual school, they could argue that this is no different to them employing somebody part-time to undertake the SENCO role and the fact that the SENCO also works in another school could even be seen as an advantage due to the experience they will have of alternative approaches. It is debatable as to whether this constitutes 'sharing' a SENCO and it is not clear that this was the intention of government guidance.

In considering these different approaches, it is useful to think about how strategic or operational the SENCO role is in a particular school. If the SENCO role is heavily operational (e.g., the day-to-day deployment of support staff), then there would be challenges in having a SENCO who was not at the school for half of the week. However, for a more strategic SENCO, there is likely to be a greater choice of possible models.

A further consideration here is that not allowing part-time workers (or others with flexible work patterns) to be SENCOs role could be deemed discriminatory. It will come back to the operational requirements of the role.

Example 2: SENCOs employed by a multi-academy trust

Where groups of schools are legally or strategically aligned (e.g., as part of a multi-academy trust or a federation), there can sometimes be one or more qualified teachers employed centrally as SENCOs, who are then deployed into the individual schools as required. The SEND Code of Practice (DfE and DoH, 2015, p 108) is clear that the 'SENCO **must** be a qualified teacher working at the school', but it is not clear whether the central deployment of SENCOs in this way fits with the intention of the code.

Some schools have interpreted the code as requiring the SENCO to be a teacher who is employed by the individual school. However, even this interpretation can be operationally problematic, since in some instances, all of the staff within a school may be employed centrally by the MAT rather than by the individual school.

An emerging model in MATs is to designate the SENCO role to a qualified teacher in each school and to have a senior central role in addition to this. Numerous job titles are used for this central role, such as Director of Inclusion, but it can be thought of as a sort of 'super SENCO'. This person can ensure that there is a common approach to inclusion across a group of schools as well as providing specialist advice, guidance, support and challenge to the SENCOs they are responsible for.

MATs with a combination of both mainstream and special schools are likely to consider how they can leverage the expertise from their specialist settings to support the MAT as a whole. One mechanism is to give the Headteacher of one of the special schools an Executive Headteacher role with responsibility for specialist provision across the MAT. This would be an alternative to having a Director of Inclusion. There are a variety of structures in place across MATs and each will have its own affordances and constraints.

Example 3: Headteacher as the SENCO

Typically, but not exclusively, the Headteacher is a qualified teacher. In a one-form entry primary school, it is likely that there will be limited financial resource available and as a consequence, the Headteacher can sometimes end up as the designated SENCO. In some instances, this is a good thing, since it means that responsibility for SEND rests with the most senior employed individual in a school, who has the authority to ensure that SEND is a strategic priority. It also means that the SENCO is on the school leadership team, which is in line with the guidance in the SEND Code of Practice if SENCOs are to be effective in the role (DfE and DoH, 2015, p 108).

Too often, however, it can be the case that the Headteacher is the SENCO in name only and the day-to-day execution of the role is delegated to another member of staff. This can end up being operationally challenging with the net effect that provision for pupils with SEND is not as good as it could be. For example, if the individual carrying out the SENCO role (without the title) does not have sufficient gravitas and status within the school, there may be unnecessary barriers to strategic progress.

There is a variation of this practice that occurs in some schools that is worthy of mention, albeit relatively uncommon. It is when the Headteacher is the designated SENCO (in name only) and the day-to-day responsibility is designated to a teaching assistant or a higher level teaching assistant. The issue with this situation is the risk of having one of the least well-qualified education professionals in a school with direct responsibility for the pupils with the most complex needs.

The essence of such debates around having a named/designated SENCO often boils down to a choice between abiding by the letter or the spirit of published guidance. There will always be loopholes and ways to avoid the intention of such guidance, but ultimately, it is there to ensure that there is a baseline level of SEND leadership infrastructure in every school. As a governor, the question to consider is whether the approach being taken is the most effective option for pupils with SEND within the constraints of the available resources. Sometimes, it can be the school's priorities rather than the overall resource limitations that have the most impact on the offer for pupils with SEND.

In situations where discussions at a board meeting descend into considering what the minimum is that a school can do to not fall foul of any particular guidance, this is where high-quality governance can robustly test strategic decisions through appropriate and targeted professional challenge. It is the role of all governors to do what is right, rather than what is easy. In situations where governors are faced with a moral dilemma in relation to decision-making (e.g., the amount of resource made available to support pupils with SEND), they may choose to apply the '3P Filter' (Schwartz, 2017, p 152).

The 3P Filter

Essentially, the 3P Filter consists of three core reflection tests designed to analyse the moral and ethical reasoning of a particular decision. These tests are as follows:

1. Public test (sometimes known as the newspaper test)
2. Parent test (sometimes known as the child test)
3. Pillow test (sometimes known as the sleep test)

The public test involves thinking about how you would feel if your decision was reported on the front page of a national newspaper. Your decision would be laid bare to the general public, which would include your friends, colleagues and family. Thought should be given as to whether you would feel comfortable knowing that you would be judged on your decision by the general public or whether such a public disclosure would bring shame or embarrassment (Schwartz, 2017, p 152).

The parent test involves thinking about what advice you would give to your own child (or another close member of the family) if they were faced with the same choice. This type of thinking can help to depersonalise the process by allowing you to remove any personal or historical 'baggage' from the scenario. This builds on the concept of separating the people from the problem (Fisher et al, 1999, p 14), which is about taking a more objective approach to solving problems by consensus. A commonly observed feature of this type of reflection is that people generally have higher expectations of their child's behaviour than they do of their own (Schwartz, 2017, p 152), which consequently raises the bar of acceptability in relation to ethical decision-making.

The pillow test is perhaps the simplest, yet most effective of the three tests. Put simply, this is about whether your decision is keeping you awake at night or whether you can sleep easily, safe in the knowledge that you have done the right thing. The good thing about this test is that it can also be retrospectively applied once the decision has been made (Schwartz, 2017, p 152). If you find that your decision is keeping you awake at night, you should consider revisiting it. There is no shame in changing your mind to put things right and some argue that this is actually a sign of strength, not weakness (Rice-Oxley, 2017). In my professional experience, people are less often judged by what happens and more often judged by what happens next.

It is fair to say that the SEND reforms of 2014 were not adequately aligned to the wider changes happening in education during the same period. The SEND reforms were eclipsed by the academisation agenda and increasing pressure on school budgets. The latter had a disproportionate impact on special schools and on mainstream schools with pupils with complex SEND because they generally had a lower ratio of staff to pupils and therefore higher staffing on-costs.

The implementation of the reforms has been challenging. Financial pressure on Local Authorities in relation to social care, for example, has coincided with increased pressure on high needs funding blocks (National Audit Office, 2019, p 30). Figure 4.2 demonstrates an upward trend in

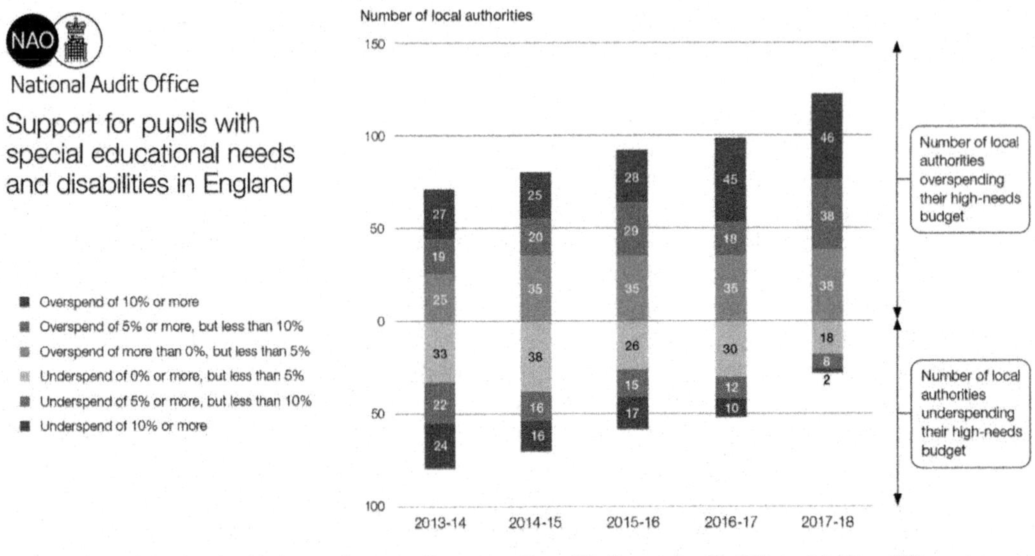

Figure 4.2 Local Authority high needs spending over time (National Audit Office, 2019, p 30).

the overspend against high needs budgets at Local Authority level. Similarly, the school accountability frameworks in place at that time (e.g., Ofsted's school inspection framework) were actively discouraging inclusive practice by focusing too heavily on academic outcomes. The SEND reforms essentially set out a commitment to identify and meet all needs in a way that worked for children and young people with SEND and their families, but this could not easily be implemented in the wider educational and financial context. Had the same set of SEND reforms been introduced a decade earlier, it is likely there would have been fewer barriers to implementation.

The SENCO role

The SEND Code of Practice (DfE and DoH, 2015, pp 108–109) outlines the statutory key responsibilities of the SENCO. In conjunction with the SENCO Induction Pack (Wharton et al, 2019), this is a useful starting point in exploring the SENCO role more broadly. As the job title suggests, the SENCO has responsibility for coordinating provision for pupils with SEND. Sometimes this will involve operational duties, but an effective SENCO should be spending the vast majority of their time working at a strategic level (Moloney, 2020, p 7).

The SEND Governor will want to sense-check the balance of operational and strategic tasks being undertaken by the SENCO. An initial indicator would be to look at whether the SENCO is part of the Senior Leadership Team in the school. This is not mandated by the SEND Code of Practice, but it is recommended they should be part of the school leadership team (DfE, 2014, p 19; DfE and DoH, 2015, p 108), and being part of the Senior Leadership Team is seen by inclusion experts as essential (Moloney, 2020, p 7). If the SENCO is an integral part of school leadership, it is much easier for them to provide effective strategic leadership (Packer, 2014, p 24). It also means that SEND provision can be built into strategic decision making from the outset rather than being retrofitted (Boddison, 2018a, p 22).

Having the SENCO on the Senior Leadership Team can be a useful way for school leaders and governors to develop a better understanding of the SENCO role. This is important because most SENCOs, particularly in secondary schools, do not feel that their role is understood by senior leaders (Curran et al, 2018, p 6). The SENCO Induction Pack (Wharton et al, 2019) is a useful accompanying document since it provides an insight into the day-to-day reality of the SENCO role for school leaders and governors. Having the SENCO on the leadership team is also a useful way to ensure they are operating in full alignment with other leaders rather than in parallel with them. In this way, the SENCO is not an isolated figure, but an in-house expert that all staff, families and learners can draw upon (Morewood, 2018, p 19).

In determining how strategic the SENCO in a school is, the SEND Governor or Headteacher (or both!) may wish to consider what the SENCO is spending their time on. The list of strategic and operational responsibilities mentioned in Table 4.1 is based on an earlier version of the Effective SENCO Deployment guide (Moloney, 2020) and whilst it is by no means exhaustive, it provides a useful starting point for such a discussion.

SENCOs and SEND Governors in special schools

The guidance in relation to the SENCO role (DfE and DoH, 2015, p 108) was intended for mainstream schools. There has never been a requirement for special schools to have a SENCO and some colleagues working in special schools would describe every teacher as being a SENCO, since they are routinely involved in provision mapping, writing individual education plans, conducting SEND assessments and contributing to EHC plans. Despite this, some special schools do choose to have SENCOs and either model can be effective.

A peculiarity of the guidance relating to SENCOs being targeted at mainstream schools is that there is, therefore, no requirement for a SENCO in a special school to have qualified teacher status or to have completed the National Award in SEN Coordination. In practice, one would hope that special schools that do appoint a SENCO ensure they are appropriately qualified.

Following an equivalent logic, there is no requirement for special schools to have a SEND Governor. If every pupil in the school has an EHC plan, then all governors are effectively SEND Governors, but again, some special schools do choose to have a designated SEND Governor with specific responsibilities.

Table 4.1 Strategic and operational responsibilities of the SENCO.

Strategic responsibilities	*Operational responsibilities*
• Ascertains whole school training needs as a result of careful analysis • Supports the senior leadership team and curriculum leaders in decisions • Liaises with curriculum leads to inform and support awareness of inclusion • Reflects on the overall profile of attendance and behaviour and considers how the school can respond and support • Ensures a framework for coproduction is in place and effective and that parental feedback is used to improve and develop inclusion • Reflects upon trends in safeguarding cases and considers changes to SEND provision in light of this • Reflects upon trends in SEND interventions and considers changes to provision in light of this • Analyses progress data by cohort to identify targeted training needs • Reflects upon financial needs and predicts potential future costs • Writes (and supports the writing of) important and statutory school documents, including the SEN Information Report and the Accessibility Plan	• Keeps the SEN register up to date • Initially assesses children coming into school • Arranges for additional resources for learners • Monitors participation levels for individual learners with SEND • Is available to parents and carers for meetings and parents' evenings • Meets with safeguarding lead(s) to review individual support needs • Line manages support staff, including monitoring performance and progress • Writes applications for high needs funding • Chairs annual reviews and completes statutory paperwork • Meets with outside agencies to support learner needs • Provides relevant updates for the school website • Provides relevant information for prospective families • Liaises with the examinations team to support access arrangements • Designs transition arrangements between schools for individual students

In order for the SEND Governor to offer appropriate support and challenge for SENCOs, it is useful for them to have a good understanding of the responsibilities of the SENCO. Table 4.2 unpacks the responsibility descriptors outlined in the SEND Code of Practice (DfE and DoH, 2015, pp 108–109).

The Headteacher role

Perhaps the most important point to make about the role of the Headteacher in relation to SEND and inclusion is that they have a central part to play. The strategic decisions that Headteachers make will impact on all students, including those with SEND. The Headteacher should work closely with the SENCO and SEND Governor to ensure there is a thorough understanding of how the school's ethos and priorities do (or do not) support inclusion.

The Headteacher should ensure that they understand the strategic and operational requirements of the SENCO role so that their line management can be as supportive and effective as possible. As stated earlier in this chapter, Headteachers are encouraged to be familiar with three specific documents published by *nasen* via Whole School SEND:

- The SENCO Induction Pack (Wharton et al, 2019)
- Effective SENCO Deployment (Moloney, 2020)
- Demonstrating Inclusion Tool: every leader a leader of SEND (Chamberlain, 2020)

As shown in Figure 4.3, Effective SENCO Deployment (Moloney, 2020, p 6) builds on the National SENCO Workload Survey (Curran et al, 2018) to identify five areas for Headteachers to focus on to maximise the impact of the SENCO. Some of these have already been discussed, but some further thought on some of the areas is included later in this chapter.

The National SENCO Workload Survey (Curran et al, 2018) showed that half of all SENCOs are on the senior leadership team, but there was a significant difference between primary schools (62%) and secondary schools (21%). More than 10% of SENCOs were also the Headteacher or Deputy Headteacher; so this raises the question of whether the SENCO would have been on the senior leadership team if the role were held by another member of staff in the school.

Table 4.2 Unpacking the responsibilities of the SENCO.

SENCO responsibility descriptors from the SEND Code of Practice (DfE and DoH, 2015, pp 108–109)	*SENCO responsibilities unpacked*
Overseeing the day-to-day operation of the school's SEN policy	• Ensuring there is regular SEND training for staff. Morewood (2018, p 19) suggests that 40% of all school inset should be SEND-related on the basis that high-quality inclusive teaching works well for all pupils, not just those with SEND. • Leading the school community to adopt inclusive values and practices (Wharton et al, 2019, p 16). This includes leading by example in order to model effective practice to the wider school community. • Ensuring there is a common understanding of inclusion across the school. • Ensuring that the overall approach to provision is designed with learners rather than done to or done for learners. • Developing the school's SEND strategy to incorporate effective preparation for adulthood, which learners want to start from the earliest years (Stobbs et al, 2018, p 3).
Co-ordinating provision for children with SEN	• Assessing the implementation and impact of provision (e.g., targeted interventions, high-quality teaching, differentiation strategies). It is important to note here that the teacher retains responsibility for provision in place for individual children in their class. The role of the SENCO is to support the teacher to be inclusive, to meet needs and to coordinate provision more strategically (e.g., identifying gaps in knowledge to inform training, linking teachers who are experienced in meeting particular SEND with those who are less experienced). • Coordination (and ongoing monitoring) of the relevant provision set out in an EHC plan or an IEP. • Having a strategic overview of the SEN support offer and how this fits within the Local Offer. • Maximising the impact of the locally available SEND expertise, including teaching assistants and other support staff. The SENCO has a key role in implementing evidence-based practice to support inclusion, such as the EEF-published report on the effective deployment of teaching assistants (Sharples et al, 2018, p 3) which recommends: o Teaching assistants should not be used as an informal teaching resource for low attaining pupils. o Use TAs to add value to what teachers do, not replace them. o Use TAs to help pupils develop independent learning skills and manage their own learning. o Ensure TAs are fully prepared for their role in the classroom. o Use TAs to deliver high-quality one-to-one and small group support using structured interventions. o Adopt evidence-based interventions to support TAs in their small group and one-to-one instruction. o Ensure explicit connections are made between learning from everyday classroom teaching and structured interventions.
Liaising with the relevant designated teacher where a looked after pupil has SEN	• Working in partnership with all designated teachers (e.g., looked after children lead, safeguarding lead, pupil premium lead). Sometimes, the same person will be responsible for more than one of these areas. Sometimes, this person is the SENCO. • Establishing with other key services beyond education (such as health or social care) whether or not greater or different input is required.
Ensuring that the school keeps the records of all pupils with SEN up to date	• Ensuring that school census data is accurate – this includes ensuring that identification is accurate and consistent right across the school. • Coordinating child-centred annual reviews for learners with EHC plans and ensuring any associated records are updated as appropriate.

(Continued)

Table 4.2 Unpacking the responsibilities of the SENCO. *(Continued)*

SENCO responsibility descriptors from the SEND Code of Practice (DfE and DoH, 2015, pp 108–109)	*SENCO responsibilities unpacked*
Advising on the graduated approach to providing SEN support	• Monitoring how teachers and others use the process of 'assess, plan, do, review' and supporting them to further improve this. • Supporting class/subject teachers on the effective implementation of SEN support. *nasen's* miniguide on SEN support and the graduated approach is clear that this is about removing barriers to learning and putting effective SEN provision in place (nasen, 2014, p 2). • Ensuring that all staff have high aspirations for all learners, particularly for those with SEND. • Ensuring there is a consistent whole school approach to SEN support (Lamb, 2018). • Ensuring there are effective professional development opportunities for staff (Packer, 2014, p 83), which are targeted, evidence-based, collaborative, sustained and evaluated (TDT, 2012; CUREE, 2011; Bolam and Weindling, 2006). • Ensuring that there is alignment between professional development opportunities and the any gaps identified in staff skills audits. • Supporting teaching staff to reflect (and improve) on the inclusiveness of their own practice. A useful tool for supporting this process is the SEND Reflection Framework (Knight, 2020). • Evaluating the effectiveness of provision for learners with SEND. Wharton et al (2019, pp 59–60) recommend lesson study (Norwich and Jones, 2014) and learning walks (see Chapter 3) as useful tools to support this process.
Advising on the deployment of the school's delegated budget and other resources to meet pupils' needs effectively	• Assessing the impact of the SEN notional budget and routinely reporting this to governors alongside pupil premium reporting. • Working with senior leaders and the SEND Governor to ensure that provision offers good value for money, is evidence based and is thoroughly evaluated (Soan, 2017, pp 26–29). • Analysing the effectiveness of costed provision through a provision map that is used to make decisions on future provision. Wharton et al (2019, p 40) suggest that this could be structured in different ways, including: o The four broad areas of need o Targeted interventions o SEN support, EHC plans o Medical needs and disabilities o Class, year group, key stage o Whole school additional needs (e.g., SEND, EAL, pupil premium, gifted and talented, looked-after children) • Assessing the impact where elements of the school budget have been allocated to SEND professional development. It is also important for SENCOs not to forget to fund, and consider the impact of, their own professional development (Packer, 2014, p 96). • Working with the SEND Governor to ensure SEND is at the heart of strategic decision-making when school budgets are discussed at board level.

Liaising with parents of pupils with SEN	• Providing a school-wide framework for meaningful coproduction to flourish. • Pro-actively reaching out to families to ensure there is family-centred partnership (Wharton et al, 2019, p 50) rather than being overly reactive. • Identifying any needs that cannot be met by the school, then working in partnership with families to request a needs assessment from the Local Authority where appropriate. • Actively urging families to encourage learners with SEND to attend your school, whilst being realistic about the available provision (it is important to avoid exclusion at the point of admission). • Detailing the provision available through an engaging SEN Information Report.
Liaising with early years providers, other schools, educational psychologists, health and social care professionals and independent or voluntary bodies Being a key point of contact with external agencies, especially the Local Authority and its support services Liaising with potential next providers of education to ensure a pupil and their parents are informed about options and a smooth transition is planned	• Developing effective partnerships and active relationships with a range of internal and external key stakeholders. • Actively engaging with local and national SEND networks (e.g., SENCO networks across the MAT/Local Authority, SEND 'teach meets', professional membership bodies like *nasen* and government-funded programmes like Whole School SEND). • Designing smooth transition arrangements between schools (and other providers such as early years settings and colleges) so that they work for all learners, including those with SEND. • Developing a sound understanding of local policies, processes and procedures so that any additional provision required for learners with SEND can be secured without undue delay. • Developing sufficient knowledge of the local, regional and national landscape of supporting organisations to be able to signpost colleagues and families as required.
Working with the Headteacher and school governors to ensure that the school meets its responsibilities under the Equality Act 2010 with regard to reasonable adjustments and access arrangements	• Attending termly meetings with SEND Governor. • Working in partnership with the Headteacher and other school leaders so that SEND is the heart of strategic decision-making (ideally as a member of the senior leadership team). • Writing the school's accessibility plan and monitoring the implementation of reasonable adjustments. • Applying for access arrangements for learners taking formal examinations. Wharton et al (2019, p 50) make the point that the national bodies responsible for overseeing access arrangements differ by setting. For primary settings, it is the STA (Standards and Testing Agency); for secondary settings, it is the JCQ (Joint Council for Qualifications); for specialist settings, it will depend on the specific qualification. Certain access arrangements do not require authorisation from the responsible national body, but the SENCO will still need to ensure the necessary arrangements are put into place.

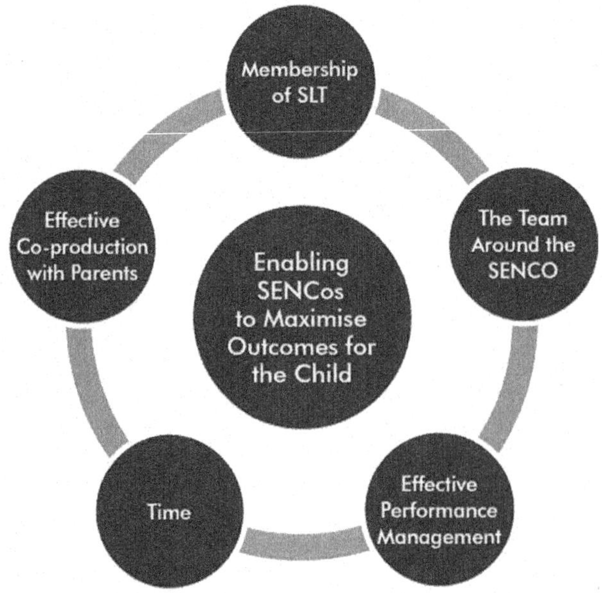

Figure 4.3 The five key themes to help maximise the impact of the SENCO (Moloney, 2020, p 6).

As the SEND Governor, if the SENCO is not a member of the senior leadership team, it is essential to ask the Headteacher to understand why that decision has been made. Sometimes, limitations of financial resources prevent the SENCO role from being a member of the senior leadership team. In such circumstances, Headteachers should actively seek to put measures in places to ensure that the SENCO has an alternative way of directly inputting into strategic decision-making. One suggestion is that they meet at least half-termly with the senior leadership team where SEND is the substantive agenda item (Moloney, 2020, p 6). Another suggestion is to share the senior leadership team meeting agendas with the SENCO in advance so they can raise any potential issues (Moloney, 2020, p10). However, the hard truth of the matter is that school leaders need their SENCO every single day (Woodley, 2017) to inform leadership decisions, so it makes good sense to simply have them on the senior leadership team.

Too many SENCOs spend the vast majority of their time on paperwork, which risks them becoming a very expensive administrator! Headteachers can support their SENCOs by giving careful thought to the team around the SENCO. This is not just about reducing the burden of administration, it is also about securing a pipeline for effective succession planning. The National SENCO Workload Survey (Curran et al, 2018) showed that only one-third of SENCOs intended to still be in the role in five years. This means there may be a 66% churn in SENCOs, which is equivalent to around 16,500 SENCOs for primary and secondary schools in England and would require 3300 new SENCOs each year.

Where practical, Headteachers should seriously consider appointing an Assistant SENCO or a Deputy SENCO since this would help both with workload and succession planning. This is also important in helping to ensure that SENCOs do not become isolated (Curran, 2019), which can happen due to their role being significantly different from that of other staff (Lewis, 2017, p 49; Parker and Bowell, 1998). The SEND Gateway has a useful role description for an Assistant SENCO, which can be accessed from https://www.sendgateway.org.uk/r/assistant-senco-role-description.html. To help tackle issues of professional isolation, Headteachers should encourage their SENCOs to join professional SEND and SENCO communities, such as *nasen* (www.nasen.org.uk) and the SENCO Forum (accessible via the SEND Gateway: https://www.sendgateway.org.uk/whole-school-send/sencos-area).

There are several other roles that operate around and interact with the SENCO role, which could be adapted to allow the SENCO to be deployed more strategically. They include teaching assistants (particularly higher level teaching assistants and those with specialist qualifications/interests), senior mental health leaders, curriculum leaders and pastoral leaders. In a MAT, the use of SENCOs as a group and the role of the Director of Inclusion could also be considered in this context. The CEOs in some MATs have chosen to appoint specialist professionals to the central team to provide strategic support, but also to be deployed into individual schools as required. These roles include Educational Psychologists, Occupational Therapists and Speech and Language Therapists.

Whilst it is clear that most SENCOs enjoy their job (Curran et al, 2018, p 7), it is also clear that they do not feel they have enough time to focus on the areas they feel can have the most impact (Curran et al, 2020, p 10). Almost all SENCOs believe they should have protected time to undertake the role and this was echoed by Headteachers in the same survey, albeit that the latter was a relatively small sample (Curran et al, 2020, p 11). The notion of protected time was also picked up by the House of Commons Education Committee with a recommendation that the Department for Education should 'commission an independent reviewer to examine the cost implications of requiring all schools and colleges to have a full-time dedicated SENCO' (House of Commons Education Committee, 2019, p 17).

The SEND Governor role

The role of the SEND Governor is to support and challenge school leaders and the wider board to make sure that priority is given to pupils with SEND getting the help they need to access the curriculum and to participate fully in the life of the school. There is no one way to ensure this happens, since the profile of needs and available resources is likely to vary significantly between schools. The SEND Governor is not personally responsible or accountable for the school's provision for learners with SEND. Rather, the entire board of governors has corporate responsibility for SEND and it can be useful to ensure this is not forgotten to avoid the burden falling unfairly on the SEND Governor or the chair.

It could be argued that every section of this book has relevance to the role of the SEND Governor, and there is no intention of summarising this entire book into a few paragraphs. Instead, it is probably more useful at this point to provide a suggested role description for the SEND Governor. This provides an outline of the expectations of the SEND Governor, but it can also be used to formally recruit a SEND Governor to your board. This is a suggested role description, which may need to be adapted for use in your particular school or context.

SEND Governor role description

Role title: SEND Governor
Responsible to: Chair of Governors
Role purpose: To monitor the school's arrangements for SEND. To provide a voice for the SENCO at board level and to ensure that the needs of learners with SEND are considered as a part of strategic decision-making. To support and challenge all senior leaders (including the SENCO) to verify that the needs of learners with SEND are being met effectively.
Duties and responsibilities:

In addition to the standard duties of effective governance, the SEND Governor role includes:

- Regular meetings with the SENCO (termly or half-termly)
- Ensuring the annual SEND report (written by school leaders) receives appropriate consideration at board level and that suitable strategic decisions are made as a consequence
- Supporting the Chair of Governors to make certain that the SEND responsibilities of the board are fully discharged
- Reminding the wider board to consider the impact of their decisions on learners with SEND, particularly where this may not be immediately obvious or explicit (recall the notion of 'Think SEND!' from Chapter 3)
- Raising SEND and inclusion issues at board level, typically in consultation with the Headteacher and the SENCO
- Monitoring the culture, values and ethos of the school to ensure they remain inclusive
- Checking that the school makes good use of financial resources (as well as the SEN notional budget) including:
    - assessing the impact of SEND spend
    - ensuring that SEND is appropriately considered in budget setting and other budget discussions
    - establishing that value for money is being achieved

- Holding the Headteacher to account in relation to:
  - the experiences of learners with SEND
  - outcomes for learners with SEND
  - the effective deployment of the SENCO and other SEND staff
- Checking the school has a designated SENCO and, if appropriate, that they have (or are working towards) the National Award for SEN Coordination as well as access to any additional training they may need.
- Direct involvement in the appointment of a new SENCO or Assistant SENCO (or trustee involvement in the appointment of a new Director of Inclusion in a MAT)
- Monitoring the SEND training received by staff and board members to ensure it is sufficient, responsive and impactful
- Checking that the board understands the school's profile of needs and that this is used to inform strategic decision-making (e.g., there should be a strong positive correlation between financial expenditure on training and the school's profile of needs)
- Ensuring the board is familiar with Chapter 6 in the SEND Code of Practice 2015
- Checking that the quality of SEND provision is good, that learners with SEND feel included and that coproduction is effective (e.g., through the coordination of SEND learning walks)
- Prompting the board to routinely check the school is compliant with key legislation, such as the Equality Act 2010 and the Children and Families Act 2014
- Ensuring the school has a high-quality SEN Information Report, Accessibility Plan and SEND Policy (if appropriate) as well as ensuring that all school policies are 'SEND-supportive'
- Requesting that data sets (e.g., attendance and progress data) presented to the board are routinely broken down to include learners with SEND, including by type of need where appropriate

In order to perform this role well, the SEND Governor is expected to:

- Attend regular training on SEND and inclusion
- Take proactive steps to remain up-to-date on the local, regional and national policy context for SEND and any associated processes and procedures
- Develop a good understanding of the school's approach to SEND provision and inclusive practice
- Be involved with the school's self-evaluation of SEND provision
- Have a thorough understanding of the views of all key stakeholders in relation to SEND (e.g., children, families, staff, volunteers, governors and the Local Authority).

Person specification:

The SEND Governor should have:

- A current role on the board as a governor (although an expert external candidate can be appointed to undertake the role as an associate governor)
- A commitment to inclusion, equality and diversity
- A commitment to learn and improve
- An interest in SEND and inclusion
- The necessary time and availability to undertake the role effectively
- Knowledge of key SEND and inclusion legislation (or a willingness to develop it)
- Professional qualifications or personal experience in SEND or inclusive education (desirable)

The role description for the SEND Governor introduces the concept of an annual SEND report for governors. There are many possible formats for such a report and below is one that is based on a template from *nasen's* Education Team.

Template for the annual SEND report for governors

School:

SENCO:

Date of report:

SEND Governor:

SEND profile for last 12 months
To include:

- *Number of pupils on SEN register (or equivalent), including numbers with Education Health and Care Plans*
- *Number of pupils on SEN register as a percentage of pupil population*
- *Number of pupils according to primary need (as on census)/gender/other characteristics, e.g., pupil premium*
- *The patterns of identification both within the school and in comparison with regional/national data*
- *Numbers of children joining the register and coming off the register this year*

Statement regarding overall quality of provision for pupils with SEND
Based on Ofsted descriptors; to include:

- *The quality of education for learners with SEND*
- *Behaviour and attitudes of learners with SEND*
- *Personal development of learners with SEND*
- *Leadership and management for SEND*

Achievement of pupils with SEND
To include:

- *Statutory assessment data*
- *School tracking data*
- *Progress data, compared to other groups and pupils with SEND regionally or nationally*
- *Wider outcomes (this may include attendance, exclusions, destinations, participation, etc.)*
- *Progress of pupils against their individual support or EHC plans*

SEN policy
When was this reviewed and have any changes been made? What was the impact?

SEN information report on school website
When was this reviewed and does it meet statutory requirements?

Statutory assessments
Use and effectiveness of access arrangements

Accessibility plan
Any updates? Review date

SEND budget and spending
What was the budget allocation and how was it spent? Value for money? Impact?

Staffing for SEND
Any staff employed specifically to support pupils with SEND

Interventions
What interventions have been used for pupils with SEND and how effective have these been? Do they offer value for money?

CPD for SEND
What CPD has taken place and what has been the impact of it for pupils with SEND?

Pupil voice
How have pupils with SEND been involved in their provision?
Satisfaction levels of pupils with SEND?

Parent/carer voice
How have parents or carers of pupils with SEND been involved?
Satisfaction levels of parents/carers of pupils with SEND?

External agencies
What external agencies have been involved and what impact has this had?

Complaints relating to SEND
Have there been any? If so, provide details

Any other developments regarding SEND?
This is an opportunity to share any other initiatives that the school has launched and what impact these have had or are hoped to have

Are there any concerns regarding provision for pupils with SEND?
This is an opportunity to share any areas that the SENCO feels may become a concern over the next year unless action is taken; this could include staffing issues, issues relating to specific pupils (without names), support from external agencies, other resourcing issues, etc.

The SEND Governor (and indeed all governors) may wish to develop a basic knowledge in relation to specific types of SEND and how schools can meet these needs. A useful resource to support this is the suite of condition-specific videos published on the SEND Gateway as part of a collaboration between the Centre for Education and Youth and Whole School SEND (CfEY, 2019). This resource is primarily aimed at newly qualified teachers to introduce them to helpful resources and tips for the classroom. However, these videos are also a good introduction to specific conditions more broadly, and they can be useful in helping the SEND Governor to identify possible questions to ask the SENCO about SEND provision at their school.

The termly meetings between the SEND Governor and the SENCO will be focused on key SEND and inclusion priorities for the school, but here is a general list of possible areas of discussion/focus:

- The current profile of SEND broken down by the four broad areas of need and numbers at the level of SEN support and EHC plans, compared with local and national averages
- Number of learners currently in the process of securing high needs funding or an EHC plan
- The engagement of children in their learning
- Any recent staff training for SEND and inclusion (delivered or attended)
- Progress on any parts of the school improvement plan relating to SEND
- The implementation of coproduction
- Evidence of compliance with statutory guidance and regulations
- Partnerships, for example, with other schools, external providers or the wider sector

It is important to remember that the SEND Governor does not line-manage the SENCO and that this is the role of the Headteacher. Instead, the SEND Governor is there to act as a critical friend to the SENCO through an appropriate balance of support and challenge. When the SENCO, the SEND Governor and the Headteacher are working effectively together, there is a genuine triangulation of SEND leadership. Table 4.3 is a useful summary of some of the key considerations for governors, Headteachers and SENCOs.

Table 4.3 SEND considerations for governors, head teachers and SENCOs.

<table>
<tr><th>Governors</th><th>Headteachers</th><th>SENCOs</th></tr>
<tr><td colspan="2">Ensure you are familiar with Chapter 6 of the SEND Code of Practice (Jan. 2015) including the 4 broad areas of need. It is 20 pages long.</td><td>Ensure you are familiar with the SEND Code of Practice (Jan. 2015). It is 292 pages long.</td></tr>
<tr><td>Ensure SEND and Pupil Premium receives similar coverage at board meetings. What is the offer for pupils who are double-disadvantaged and triple-funded?</td><td>Consider the deployment of the SENCO. Could they focus more on high-quality teaching and less on paperwork?</td><td>Think about how to progress through the stages of coproduction (done to, done for, done with) and how to embed the 'graduated approach'.</td></tr>
<tr><td colspan="2">Use profile of need to inform strategic decision making (e.g., resource allocation and CPD priorities). Is our school a 'SEND magnet'?</td><td>Use profile of need data to probe the accuracy of identification (and reduce exclusions) and to inform targeted small-group interventions.</td></tr>
<tr><td colspan="3">Would you feel confident in articulating why your school (and its curriculum) is inclusive? Is this intent for inclusion consistently understood (including by families)?</td></tr>
<tr><td>Is your school fully compliant with statutory guidance (in particular, the SEND Code of Practice 2015 and the Equality Act 2010). Ensure your school has a high quality, accessible SEN Information Report</td><td colspan="2">What does it mean for students with SEND to 'achieve exceptionally well' in your school? Is this only about academic outcomes?</td></tr>
<tr><td colspan="2">Ensure that SEND is 'built in' to your school improvement plans and not a 'bolt-on'. Undertaking SEND reviews at a range of levels could inform this.</td><td>Ensure that teaching assistants are being deployed effectively (e.g., how much teacher-time do learners with SEND receive?)</td></tr>
<tr><td colspan="3">Familiarise yourself with the SENCO Induction Handbook to ensure a triangulated approach to SEND leadership.</td></tr>
</table>

Summary

This chapter was focused on introducing the concept of the triangle of SEND Leadership: the SENCO, the Headteacher and the SEND Governor. It explored some of the practicalities of the SEND Governor's role. Having read this chapter, you should now have developed your knowledge and understanding of:

- How the SENCO, Headteacher and SEND Governor can collaborate for effective leadership of SEND
- Alternative approaches to the deployment of the SENCO
- The role of the 3P Filter for moral dilemmas in strategic decision-making
- The strategic and operational responsibilities of the SENCO
- The duties and responsibilities of the SEND Governor

The ten key messages that should be taken from this chapter are:

1. **The SEND Governor is not personally responsible or accountable for the school's provision for learners with SEND.** The entire board of governors has corporate responsibility for SEND.
2. **The SEND Governor is a critical friend to the SENCO – not their line manager.** The SENCO's line manager would typically be the Headteacher, particularly if the SENCO is part of the senior leadership team. The SEND Governor can be an advocate for the SENCO at board level and they should provide the SENCO with an appropriate balance of support and challenge to ensure the needs of learners are being met.
3. **The SENCO is most effective when they are part of the school leadership team** (DfE and DoH, 2015, p 108). The SEND Governor should be making the case to the Headteacher and the wider board for this to happen. If the SENCO is not on the school leadership team, it is important that there is a mechanism for them to contribute directly to strategic decision making.
4. **The Director of Inclusion role in a MAT is most effective when it is in addition to, and not instead of, SENCOs in individual schools.** Whilst there are some circumstances in which sharing a SENCO between schools is necessary, this should be the exception rather than the rule. Each school should have its own dedicated SENCO, and the addition of a Director of Inclusion can be useful when growing the strategic capacity of SEND expertise across a MAT.
5. **The SENCO should be spending the vast majority of their time on strategic rather than operational matters.** The SEND Governor might want to explore how strategically the Headteacher is deploying the SENCO. If the SENCO is spending most of their time on paperwork, the risk is that they become a very expensive administrator.
6. **There is no requirement for special schools to have a SENCO or a SEND Governor, but when they do, they should be appropriately qualified.** Since all of the learners in a special school are likely to have EHC plans, it could be argued that SEND provision is the top priority for all governors. Similarly, teachers in special schools are likely to be routinely involved with tasks associated with SENCOs in mainstream schools, such as provision mapping, writing individual education plans, conducting SEND assessments and contributing to EHC plans.
7. **The SEND Governor should ensure that coproduction is happening and that it is effective.** Careful consideration needs to be given as to how family views on coproduction are captured and considered at board level.
8. **The SEND Governor should meet at least termly with the SENCO.** Visits should have a clear agenda and be purposeful with a report of the visit, and any associated recommendations, presented for discussion at the next board meeting.
9. **School leaders and SENCOs should aim for at least 40% of staff training and professional development to be SEND-related** (Morewood, 2018, p 19). This is on the basis that high-quality inclusive teaching that works well for learners with SEND is likely to work well for all learners.
10. **The SEND Governor should support the SENCO to produce an annual SEND report for governors.** The SEND Governor can ensure that recommendations from the SENCO receive appropriate consideration at board level and that suitable strategic decisions are made as a consequence.

5 Using data strategically to develop SEND provision and evaluate effectiveness

The aim of this chapter is to consider how data can be used to get a sense of how inclusive a school is. As discussed in Chapter 1, inclusion can mean different things to different people, so the first step is for the board to consider what it means to be an inclusive school in their specific context. Governors are responsible for establishing the culture, ethos and values of the school, all of which will help to develop a shared notion of inclusion.

Frameworks for inclusion

Ofsted has set out three broad expectations of schools in relation to developing an inclusive culture, stating that schools should:

- identify early those pupils who may be disadvantaged or have additional needs or barriers to learning
- meet the needs of those pupils, drawing, when necessary, on more specialist support, and help those pupils to engage positively with the curriculum
- ensure pupils have a positive experience of learning and achieve positive outcomes.

(Ofsted, 2019b, p 69)

This is useful in that it establishes a basic framework for discussing and articulating the specific elements of an inclusive culture for a school. There are also several other well-established frameworks for inclusion from across the UK and Europe that boards may wish to use, such as:

- Inclusion Quality Mark (McCann and McCann, 2004)
- Index for Inclusion (Booth and Ainscow, 2011)
- Inclusive Education Framework (NCSE, 2014)
- National Framework for Inclusion (STEC, 2014)
- The CIRCLE Framework – Secondary (Education Scotland, 2019)
- Participation in Inclusive Education: A Framework (EADSNE, 2011)

The *Index for Inclusion* is probably the most widely-used of these frameworks having been translated into 37 languages and used in 35 countries (Pillay et al, 2015, p 8). The index begins by considering the indicators of an inclusive culture and this flows directly into inclusive policies and inclusive practices as follows:

- **Dimension A: Creating inclusive cultures**
  - Building community
  - Establishing inclusive values
- **Dimension B: Producing inclusive policies**
  - Developing the school for all
  - Organising support for diversity
- **Dimension C: Evolving inclusive practices**
  - Orchestrating learning
  - Mobilising resources

A more detailed breakdown of the indicators can be found on the Centre for Studies in Inclusive Education website: http://www.csie.org.uk/resources/inclusion-index-explained.shtml#indicators.

A common challenge with some of these frameworks for inclusion is that they are overly-reliant on qualitative data that can be more subjective in nature than quantitative data (Pickell, 2019). For example, a policy that is deemed inclusive by one person may be deemed to be non-inclusive by another. This happens because they have differing personal experiences and value-bases that inform their perspectives. Similarly, a teaching and learning practice deemed inclusive in one school may be deemed non-inclusive in another school.

It can be tempting to tackle this perceived subjectivity by seeking out quantitative metrics, which are arguably more objective. The problem is that there is no universally accepted way to measure inclusion and there is limited, if any, consensus on what a possible dashboard of quantitative measures for inclusion should consist of. Despite this, there is a whole range of metrics, based on data that schools already collect, which can provide an insight into the overall inclusiveness of a school. The individual metrics do not measure inclusion, but considered together as 'indicators of inclusion', they are arguably a useful set of proxy measures. Such metrics may include data on unauthorised absence, exclusions and progress/attainment.

Indicators of inclusion

In making the decision about what metrics might be useful indicators of inclusion and therefore ought to be part of an inclusion dashboard, it is worth noting the risk of unintended consequences. A particular risk is that governors and school leaders become focused on improving the specific metrics being measured rather than the inclusiveness of the provision that underpins them. This is perhaps a broader issue about the current culture of our education system, where quality measures are too often confused with quality itself (Biesta, 2014). The aim should be to measure what we value, known as normative validity, rather than to value what is measurable, known as technical validity (Biesta, 2014; Ball, 2003).

A second risk is that when data is used for benchmarking a school against other schools or regional/national data, there can be an underlying assumption of comparing like-with-like. However, the reality is that every school is contextually different, so whilst these comparisons can provide useful insights, there are validity limitations in drawing conclusions on the basis of data alone. There may also be legitimate contextual reasons why a particular data set looks the way it does and it may therefore be wholly inappropriate for it to emulate the national picture. However, drawing out these differences and discussing them is a good way for governors to develop their understanding of the contextual nuance associated with their schools.

Thirdly, there is a risk of aspiring to achieve some 'perfect data set' that shows the school has excelled in its approached inclusion and has got it right for all learners. The truth about inclusion is that the job is never completed as there is always more that can be done. This does not mean that the school is not inclusive; it means it can always be more inclusive. In the words of the ethics expert, Michael Josephson, 'you don't have to be sick to get better' (Josephson, 2001).

Despite these risks, governors and school leaders can use existing data to get an insight into how inclusive their schools are, particularly if they consider the data as one input from a wider set of considerations. The measures should not be seen as outcomes in and of themselves, but rather as a mechanism for focusing strategic discussion. Time for detailed data analysis can be limited in board meetings, so using an 'inclusion dashboard' can be a good way of establishing a set of targeted questions for governors to ask and for developing any lines of inquiry for the school to pursue further beyond the meeting.

The next section of this chapter will consider a range of different data sets in turn and the type of insights that could be gleaned from them in relation to inclusion.

Unauthorised absence

School leaders routinely monitor attendance rates for pupils and by association this will include absence rates. Governors will typically receive summaries of this data and this should ideally include a breakdown of the data by the different levels of SEN provision. At a national level, there has been a persistent 4% gap in absence rates between pupils without SEN and those with the most complex needs (i.e., those with an EHC plan or, prior to 2014, a statement) as shown in Figure 5.1 (DfE, 2020a, p 16).

This is not surprising since a significant proportion of learners with EHC plans have medical needs or other needs that require them to be out of school to access the therapeutic interventions and services they need. Perhaps more worrying is the persistent 2% gap in absence rates between pupils without SEN and those at the level of SEN support.

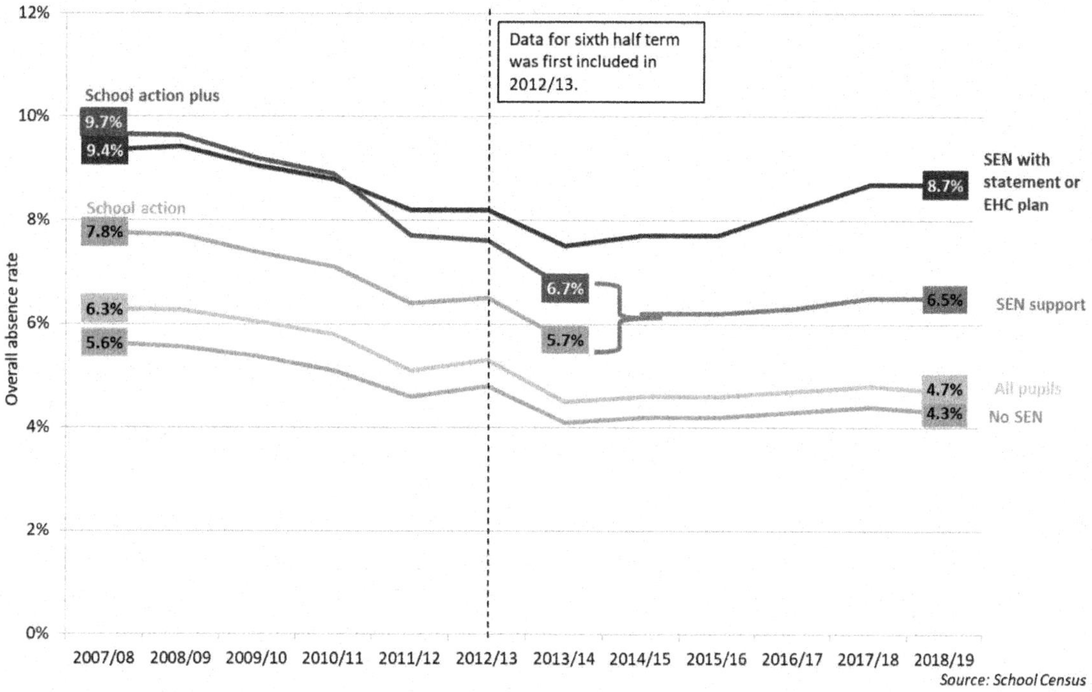

Figure 5.1 Percentage of sessions missed over time by SEN level (DfE, 2020a, p 16).

Governors should ensure they ask questions that help them to understand why learners with SEND are not attending school as regularly as learners without SEND. One way of getting more quickly to the heart of the issue is to ask for data on unauthorised absences, rather than absence more broadly. This will remove the 'legitimate' absences, such as hospital appointments, from the data and could expose any underlying attendance issues. For example, if a large proportion of unauthorised absence consists of learners with SEND, this may suggest that more can be done to make the school experience work better for them.

Governors may want to ask whether the pupils with the highest levels of unauthorised absences have any needs in common. For example, if most of the unauthorised absence was linked to say SEMH, this may be an area that the school could focus on providing more support to increase attendance. SEMH more broadly may then become an area where governors subsequently want to increase their scrutiny through more targeted support and challenge.

The underlying question for governors to consider is whether the unauthorised absence of pupils with SEND is a consequence of the school failing to meet the needs of those pupils. At the individual pupil level, this could be about reasonable adjustments that need to be put into place. At the strategic level, which is where the governor focus should be, this could be about unintended consequences of particular policies, practices or the overall ethos of the school.

For example, a secondary school may have a behaviour policy that insists on 'silent corridors' or that 'pupils look teachers in the eye when speaking to them'. For learners with certain types of SEND, adhering to such rules may be traumatic or even impossible. One could easily foresee a scenario where learners refuse to come to school because they do not want to get in trouble and because the experience of school has a negative emotional effect on them. In short, they feel unwelcome and the school is not inclusive. Governors need to ask the right questions so they understand the operational consequences of the policies they approve and the ethos they establish. They are then in a position to address any issues that arise and to further establish inclusion at the school. Governors will also want to be assured that the school's policies are not being used for off-rolling.

Exclusions

The long-standing disproportionately high rate of exclusions for learners with SEND compared to learners without SEND is well documented (Tirraoro, 2018; Timpson, 2019, p 36; McGill, 2020). Data published in 2019 (DfE, 2019) shows that learners at SEN support are significantly more likely to be permanently excluded than learners without SEND. Similarly, learners at SEN support are four and a half times more likely to receive fixed term exclusion than learners without SEND.

An analysis of the data for permanently excluded learners with SEND shows that 61% had a primary need of SEMH. There is a similar trend for fixed term exclusions where 53% of excluded learners had a primary need of SEMH (DfE, 2019). This alone is reason enough for governors to be asking questions about the effectiveness of provision for learners with SEMH needs and the impact of resources that are being targeted at this important group.

Governors should be asking for data on fixed term and permanent exclusions together with bench-marking against local and national data for comparison. The data should ideally span multiple years so that trends can be identified. In particular, governors will want to be assured that the gap between exclusions for learners with SEND and for learners without SEND is narrowing, and that exclusions overall are reducing. The board should consider whether any of their policies could be strengthened to help avoid exclusions.

Where exclusions do occur, it is important to note that that boards have an important role to play in challenging exclusions that may be ethically dubious. In particular, governors should look to school leaders to assure them that exclusions are not happening as a direct consequence of unmet needs.

Example of an ethically dubious exclusion of a pupil with ADHD

Consider the situation where a pupil with ADHD is struggling to remain in his/her seat during lessons. The teacher may repeatedly ask the pupil to sit down, but his/her ADHD needs may be such that he/she cannot comply with this request. If this continues over an extended period, the school may deem this to be persistent disruptive behaviour and the pupil could be excluded.

If the school had not put appropriate support in place (e.g., movement breaks or breaking learning tasks into smaller chunks), it would then be grossly unfair for the pupil to be excluded. Governors need to establish that effective support was in place, since not having this support would be both morally wrong as well as grounds for successfully appealing an exclusion.

Progress and attainment

When school leaders share progress and attainment data with governors, they can sometimes include a 'shadow' set of data, which is essentially what the data would look like if the data for learners with SEND was not included. Whilst the rationale for this can come from wanting to demonstrate that most learners are making good progress and achieving well, this approach is problematic for a number of reasons:

- It can give the impression that learners with SEND are a burden on overall progress and attainment. The accountability pressures on schools are such that what starts out as a simple variation in the presentation of the data can slowly erode the inclusive culture of a school.
- It can suggest that the school is embarrassed or uncomfortable about the progress and attainment for learners with SEND. Rather than presenting a shadow data that excludes learners with SEND, it would better for the original data set to demonstrate pride in what has been achieved. For example:
  - Are progress rates for learners with SEND increasing?
  - What proportion of learners with EHC plans are on track to achieve the targets set out in their plans?
  - How do the attainment rates for learners with SEND in the school compare with local and national averages or with other similar schools?
- It assumes that learners with SEND cannot achieve the same levels of progress and achievement as those without SEND. There should be high aspirations for all pupils and it is worth remembering that for learners with DME and for those whose needs are not related to cognition and learning, good support will enable them to achieve as well as learners without SEND.

Whatever approach schools choose to take in respect of the data they present to the board, the underlying principle should be based on valuing a broad set of outcomes and celebrating the achievements of all learners. It is useful to have a breakdown of progress and attainment data by complexity or type of SEND, since this will allow governors to compare different groups and to verify that the school's approach is working for all groups of learners. However, it is less useful (and arguably problematic) to have data sets that exclude specific subsets of the overall pupil population to present a more positive picture.

In considering what governors and trustees need to know about the progress and attainment of children with SEND, here are five key questions they should have discussed and know the answers to (nasen and NGA, 2018):

1. How successful is the school in meeting the needs of learners with SEND so they achieve good outcomes?
2. How do you know?
3. If outcomes are not good, is this a resourcing issue? (e.g., staff capacity, competence, access to professional development, classroom resources or equipment).
4. What are the barriers to further improvement and even better outcomes for learners with SEND?
5. What actions could the board take to ensure that priorities address any barriers and challenges concerning SEND?

Census data

In January each year, schools complete the annual census return, part of which involves providing information about the profile of SEND within the pupil population. This data is then aggregated and published by the DfE in July each year (DfE, 2007–2019). The published data is available by Local Authority or at the national level, and both are useful benchmarks when considering the distribution of needs for an individual school.

At the most basic level, governing bodies should look at the proportion of pupils with SEND at the school and compare this with local and national averages. This includes considering the prevalence of learners with no SEND, those at SEN support and those with EHC plans. As discussed in Chapter 1, this will help to determine if the school is a SEND magnet or if it is attracting fewer learners with SEND than other local schools. It will also provide a mechanism for governors to become aware if their schools are failing to identify SEND where it exists within their pupil population.

To be clear, it is not a requirement (nor is it realistic) that the proportion of learners with SEND in each school should mirror local or national averages exactly. However, when governors are aware of any significant variations, they can target their boardroom questions to shine a light on the reasons why this might be the case. Table 5.1 considers three common scenarios where the data might highlight a difference and provide some questions that governors could ask to probe further.

The answers to the above questions can be considered alongside other data, such as feedback from families, to build a picture of the ethos of SEND and inclusion at the school. For example, if census data show the school has fewer children with SEND, but there are complaints from families that their children are not having their needs met, this might suggest the school is under-identifying needs. By building their understanding in this way, governors can find the right balance of support and challenge and can use the intelligence to inform their strategic decision making.

Also available within these statistics is the proportion of learners with SEND by primary area of need. Governors can be presented with data comparing their own school against local and national data. As stated previously, this is not about conforming to local or national averages, but where there are differences, it is good to understand the reasons for this. Governors need to assure themselves that the available resources are appropriately aligned to the school's profile of needs.

To get an idea of how this might work in practice, here is an example of how a fictitious school from Blackpool, Lady Videtta High School, might use a particular set of published census data.

A governor or a school leader at Lady Videtta High School analysing this data by looking at Figure 5.2 and Table 5.2 might consider the following:

1. The proportion of learners with Moderate Learning Difficulties, Other Difficulty/Disability or SEN support with no specialist assessment of type of need is higher at Lady Videtta High School than it is locally. These three areas of need are similar in that they can sometimes be inappropriately used as broad 'catch-all' type categories. This suggests that accurate

Table 5.1 Governor questions about the proportion of learners with SEND.

Scenario	*Governor questions*
The overall proportion of children with SEND at the school is significantly higher than local and national averages	• Are there more learners with SEND at this school than other schools or has the school been more effective at identifying needs? How do you know? • What measures has the school put in place to ensure that the identification of SEND is accurate? • Are there any moderation (or other) processes in place to improve the reliability of assessment of SEND and to ensure alignment with other local schools? • How does the proportion of learners with SEND at the school vary over time (e.g., 3-year trend data) and how does this compare with local/national data?
The overall proportion of children with SEND at the school is significantly lower than local and national averages	• Are there fewer learners with SEND at this school than other schools or has the school been more effective at meeting needs? How do you know? • How confident are teachers at identifying SEND, adapting their teaching and liaising with the SENCO where additional support may be required? • What is the local reputation of the school in relation to inclusion and meeting the needs for learners with SEND? Are potential parents/carers confident the school can meet the needs of their child? • Is the school's admissions process as inclusive as it could be? How does the school know that learners with SEND are not being excluded at the point of admission or beforehand?
The proportion of children at SEN support at the school is significantly higher than local averages, but the proportion with EHC plans is significantly lower	• Are school leaders confident that the significantly higher proportion of learners at SEN support is not due to a lack of high quality inclusive teaching (quality-first teaching)? • How many learners has the school supported to secure a needs assessment from the Local Authority? What proportion of these resulted in an EHC plan being issued? • What is the school's SEN support offer? Is it adequate in meeting the volume and complexity of needs? • What training and CPD have teachers had over the past two years to support them in meeting the needs of learners with SEND?

Table 5.2 Analysis by primary area of need – Lady Videtta High School.

	Proportion of learners by primary area of need (%)													
	Specific Learning Difficulty	Moderate Learning Difficulty	Severe Learning Difficulty	Profound & Multiple Learning Difficulty	Social, Emotional and Mental Health	Speech, Language and Communications Needs	Hearing Impairment	Visual Impairment	Multi-Sensory Impairment	Physical Disability	Autistic Spectrum Disorder	Other Difficulty/Disability	SEN support but no specialist assessment of type of need	Total
Lady Videtta High School	4.7	29.5	0.0	0.0	25.7	23.8	1.3	1.2	0.8	0.3	2.9	4.1	5.7	100
Blackpool	5.6	23.2	0.3	0.0	21.0	39.0	1.3	1.1	0.8	2.7	3.2	1.4	0.4	100
England	9.5	20.9	0.6	0.3	16.3	30.6	1.7	0.9	0.3	2.8	7.9	3.9	4.3	100

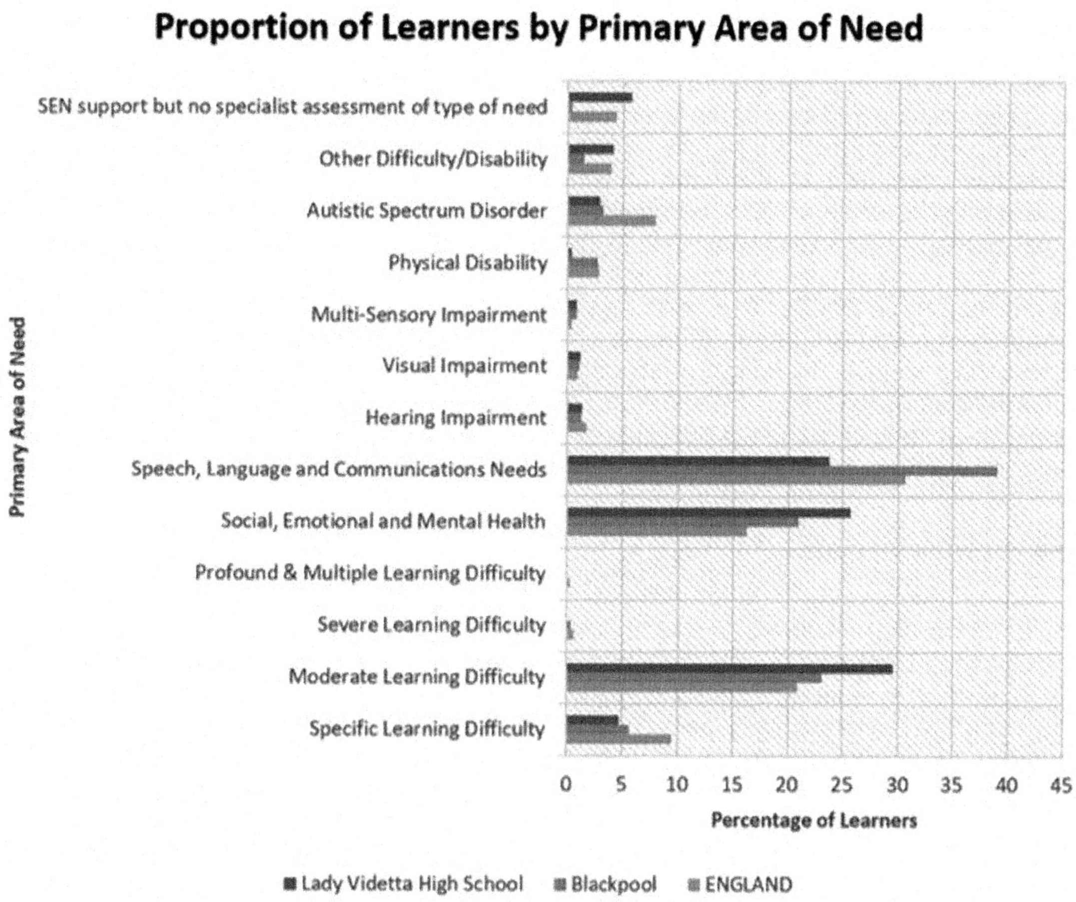

Figure 5.2 Analysis by primary area of need – Lady Videtta High School.

identification of needs may be an issue at Lady Videtta High School and should be explored further. That being said, two of these areas are in line with national data, so part of the issue may be to do with local approaches to identification rather than the school itself. It is also notable that the proportion of learners with Speech, Language and Communication Needs is lower than both Blackpool and England. Could it be that some of those learners with a broader identification of SEND (e.g., Moderate Learning Difficulties) actually have unidentified Speech, Language and Communication Needs? Do the processes for identifying these needs have an appropriate level of validity and reliability and specialist input?

2. The proportion of learners with Social, Emotional and Mental Health needs is higher at Lady Videtta High School than Blackpool and England. What provision does the school have in place to support wellbeing and what does this data suggest about the effectiveness of this provision? Is the school confident that unidentified, and therefore unmet, needs are not becoming anxiety issues over time? Are there any particular groups of learners who are most at risk of developing Social, Emotional and Mental Health difficulties and are school resources aligned to addressing this?
3. The proportion of learners with Autism Spectrum Disorder is in line with local data, but significantly below national data. From a positive perspective, it may be that autism provision at the school and locally is highly effective, with many learners having their needs met and therefore not being recorded as having SEND on the census. However, governors will want to assure themselves that there is not a significant under-identification of autism needs here. From a more challenging perspective, it may be that the families do not have confidence in the local autism provision and are actively choosing to send their children to schools outside the area.

This is an example of the type of discussions that governors can have to help them better understand where barriers to inclusion may exist and it can support school leaders in considering their approach to the deployment of the SENCO and other SEND resources.

A consistency issue that can arise is the process for determining the criteria for inclusion on the SEN register. Some schools take the view that a learner is added to the register only if he/she requires provision that is 'different from or additional to' that which is normally provided for all learners. Others will take the view that all learners with formally identified needs should always be recorded even if those needs are already being met by high quality inclusive teaching. Governors should check that school leaders and SENCOs have measures in place to ensure there is consistency within their school and at a local level. This will increase the validity and reliability of the census data, particularly at the level of SEN support.

When considering trends over time for either the prevalence of SEND in general or of specific needs, it is important to do this in the context of the wider demographic changes of educational provision. For example, in 2010, pupils with SEN without a statement were fairly evenly spread across primary and secondary schools (51.4% and 43.6%, respectively) with 4% in independent schools, 0.7% in pupil referral units and 0.1% in special schools (UCL CIE and Firmament Education, 2019, p 29). By 2018, there had been a significant divergence between primary and secondary schools with 57.1% of pupils at SEN support in primary schools and only 33.9% in secondary schools. Independent schools, pupil referral units and special schools have all increased steadily to 7.1%, 1.1% and 0.3%, respectively. This suggests there could be a national identification issue in relation to SEN support in our secondary schools, which should be taken into consideration when considering the census data at school level.

Environmental data

Boards will routinely receive data and reports that provide an insight to the physical environment of the school. This could include the outcome of health and safety visits, financial requests for expenditure on essential maintenance/upgrades, analyses of accident reporting or the accessibility plan. The physical environment can be a key factor in making schools more inclusive, so governors should take the opportunity to consider what all of these data sets are telling them.

For example, if learners with SEND accounted for a disproportionately high number of accidents at the school, governors should explore with the Headteacher why that is the case. It may be that the health and safety signage is inaccessible to learners with certain types of need. It may be targeted interventions are routinely delivered at a time (such as assembly) when learners would typically receive messages about the safe use of outdoor spaces, so they end of up missing them. Whatever the reason, this is an opportunity for governors to challenge why accident rates are high for learners with SEND and to offer support to help it to reduce.

Similarly, when budget requests for maintenance and upgrades are received, this provides an opportunity to consider whether the school environment can become more accessible and inclusive. Governors can ask what the benefit of the expenditure will be for learners with SEND and whether there could be any unintended consequences. This goes back to the principle of 'Think SEND!' established in Chapter 2.

Financial data

Governors typically receive plentiful financial data, but it is not always used as a mechanism to support and challenge the school's offer in relation to SEND and inclusion. As discussed in Chapter 2, it is important for governors to know what the school's SEN notional budget is, how it is being spent and the impact of that spend on learners with SEND (particularly at the level of SEN support). Other areas of financial data related to SEND and inclusion that governors may want to know more about could be:

- Impact of expenditure on SEND-related training and CPD for staff and volunteers
- Cost of teaching assistants tracked against SEND prevalence over time
- Value for money in relation to any external specialist provision, including benchmarking against other similar schools

If governors have any concerns about what is being spent on SEND (or not), it is something that can also be picked up as part of internal or external audit processes should that be deemed appropriate.

Pipeline and destinations data

Data analysis in schools is typically focused on school-centric data, which is completely understandable. However, there is some value in considering the pupil data from the phases before and after your particular school setting – pipeline data and destinations data.

Secondary schools often draw a large proportion of their intake from the same group of primary schools and the same local area(s). It would be beneficial for secondary school SENCOs to use the published census data to consider the profiles of needs in local primary schools, so they can make strategic preparations for the cohorts they are likely to receive in future years. In this way, secondary schools can be proactive rather than reactive in relation to staff training and resource allocation.

Similarly, primary schools may wish to consider the data published in relation to SEND in the early years. Primary SENCOs should be familiar with local trends in the proportion of children with SEN achieving a good level of development in the early years, which was only 25% nationally in 2018/2019 (DfE, 2020a, p 10). By considering the effectiveness of their current provision for learners with SEND in foundation stage two and year one alongside the trends in the early years, primary SENCOs can assess what more needs to be put in place for future cohorts and what support they may be able to offer to early years settings.

Special schools perhaps have the most difficult role in relation to pipeline data, since they can be structured by need rather than year group. This means they may need to consider data from many different sources. Conversely, the enhanced level of specialist provision arguably means they are better prepared to meet a more diverse and complex range of needs in the first place. Nevertheless, it is still important for special schools to be proactive in considering any pipeline data available to them.

The consideration of destinations data is mainly about helping schools to understand the impact of their current provision. For primary settings, this is a relatively straightforward process in that it is generally confined to the type of setting that learners transition to next. Success is not determined by what proportions of children go on to particular types of setting, but rather by whether they have transitioned to a setting that they wanted and that can meet their needs.

For special schools and secondary schools, the destinations data is weighted more towards a measure of effective preparation for adulthood. There is published data in relation to the proportion of 16- and 17-year-olds in education and training, their destinations six months after completing key stage five and the proportion of learners with SEND who progress to university (DfE, 2020a, p 14). Again, special schools and secondary schools will know their learners well and will have data on whether learners are satisfied that their educational experience has adequately prepared them for what they want to do next.

Whilst the data analysis will be done by the SENCO and Headteacher (or a data officer for larger schools) rather than by governors, this should be shared at board level. This ensures that governors have a more nuanced understanding of SEND and provision, and that they can seek to make decisions that will 'lock in' learning at a strategic level. In the context of Covid-19, all boards should be thinking about how to 'lock in' any learning in relation to what has improved inclusion during the period of blended and remote curriculum delivery (Swaithes et al, 2020).

Going beyond the indicators

Whilst a few possible indicators of inclusion have been suggested above, this is clearly only a small subset of the data available in a school. There may well be other datasets that are useful to consider too. To help with this, the European Agency for Development in SEN has published a framework to support education providers to identify and develop new indicators (EADSNE, 2011, pp 38–40).

Five-stage process for developing new indicators of inclusion (EADSNE, 2011, pp 38–40)

- Step 1: Make an inventory of available data
- Step 2: Identify gaps in available data
- Step 3: Check whether available data can be aggregated and disaggregated across levels
- Step 4: Check whether available data can be monitored across the process of education
- Step 5: Check whether available data respects the interests of the persons behind the data

Remember that schools can collect and generate additional data for any areas they identify as gaps. In Chapter 2, the concept of using surveys to gather the views of key stakeholders was discussed. This kind of data is highly complementary to the indicators discussed above. Additional data sets that may be of value to generate could be:

- Stakeholder views from surveys (children, families, staff and volunteers)
- Rates of attendance/participation at school events, including families of children with SEND (EADSNE, 2011, p 29)
- Proportion of complaints/compliments about provision that are SEND-related
- Confidence of teachers in meeting SEND needs
- Proportion of teachers recognised for inclusion (e.g., having achieved *nasen's* Recognised Teacher of SEND)
- Analysis of SEND-related social media engagement (note that this may be time consuming or require specialist software)

Once governors have a full understanding of SEND and inclusion in their school and they have considered the wealth of data analysis available to them, it is possible that they will identify a long list of areas they would like to develop and improve. There will be some areas that are beyond the influence of governors, such as national policy and school funding levels, and there will be some areas in which the risks or the costs of development outweigh the potential benefits. In deciding which areas of improvement to prioritise, governors might consider the advice that battles should be small enough to win, but big enough to make a difference. Ultimately, the overall role of governors and trustees in relation to SEND and inclusion can be summed up in just eight words. In the words of Hannah Moloney (2020a) governors and trustees should ensure that:

"No child is missed"

&

"No child misses out"

Summary

This chapter considered how data can be used at board level to get a sense of how inclusive a school is and to develop a shared notion of inclusion. Having read this chapter, you should have now developed your knowledge and understanding of:

- The different frameworks for inclusion available to schools
- The indicators of inclusion that governors can draw upon
- Published data sets that can be used for benchmarking
- The value of pipeline and destinations data
- The process for identifying new indicators of inclusion and developing additional data sets

The ten key messages that should be taken from this chapter are:

1. **Governors should ensure there is a shared notion of what inclusion means for their school.** This notion should be coproduced with children, families, staff and volunteers.
2. **There is no one metric for measuring inclusion.** Inclusion is a complex concept and getting a sense of it requires considering a range of quantitative and qualitative indicators.
3. **High levels of unauthorised absence amongst pupils with SEND should be explored by governors.** This could be an indication that the school is not inclusive or inaccessible for some learners with SEND.
4. **Boards should know what actions they can take to support the removal of barriers and challenges for learners with SEND.** Governors should regularly assure themselves that the school's policies and ethos are not inadvertently driving non-inclusive behaviours.
5. **Governors should consider school data in the context of local and national data.** Benchmarking data and the trends in schools over time will both be key factors in appropriately interpreting school data.
6. **School data should always be considered in the context of feedback from families, not in isolation.** To ensure that provision is child-centred, effective coproduction should be in place so the wishes of children and their families are considered alongside school data.

7. **Governors should use data on the physical school environment as an opportunity to champion greater inclusion.** Developments to the school infrastructure should work for all learners and every improvement should make the school more inclusive.
8. **Governors should ensure there is value for money on SEND spend.** With limited funding available, value for money is more important than ever. Governors could consider asking the school to undertake a cost-benefit analysis of SEND spend.
9. **Battles should be small enough to win, but big enough to make a difference.** School's must prioritise as they do not have the capacity to do everything at once. This mantra is a useful and quick test of suitability for emerging priorities.
10. **Ultimately, governors should ensure that 'no child is missed' and that 'no child misses out'** (Moloney, 2020a). This is not for governors to carry out directly, but they should create the culture and ethos for this to happen in their school.

References

Baker, W. and King, H. (2013) Participatory learning walks: Reflective practice for the conductor-music educator. *Australian Journal of Music Education*. Vol. 2, pp 35–45.

Ball, S.J. (2003) The teacher's soul and the terrors of performativity. *Journal of Education Policy*. Vol. 18, pp 215–228.

Bartram, D. and Patel, V. (2020) *SEND review guide*. https://www.sendgateway.org.uk/whole-school-send/find-wss-resources/ Accessed in April 2020.

BBC (2012) *Ofsted says poor pupils losing out on 'premium' funds*. https://www.bbc.co.uk/news/education-19649306/ Accessed in May 2020.

Biesta, G. (2014) Measure what we value or value what we measure? Globalization, responsibility and the notion of purpose of education. Educational thought. *Latin American Educational Research Journal.* Vol. 51, *No.*1, *pp* 46–57.

Boddison, A. (2018) *Special educational needs review 2018*. In Schools Week (2018) https://schoolsweek.co.uk/special-educational-needs-review-2018/ Accessed in November 2019.

Boddison, A. (2018a) SEND Leadership. In Bartram, D., *Great Expectations: Leading an Effective SEND Strategy in School.* John Catt: Woodbridge.

Boddison, A. (2019) *Does Ofsted's draft inspection framework pass the inclusion test?* In Schools Week https://schoolsweek.co.uk/does-ofsteds-draft-inspection-framework-pass-the-inclusion-test/ Accessed in December 2019.

Bolam, R. and Weindling, D. (2006) *Synthesis of Research and Evaluation Projects Concerned With Capacity-Building Through Teachers' Professional Development*. GTCE: London, UK.

Booth, T. and Ainscow, M. (2011) *Index for Inclusion: Developing Learning and Participation in Schools*. Third Edition. Centre for Inclusive Education: Bristol, UK.

Centre for Studies in Inclusive Education (2018) *Social and educational justice – The human rights framework for inclusion*. http://www.csie.org.uk/resources/soc-ed-justice.shtml Accessed in January 2020.

CfEY (2019) *Condition-specific videos*. Created by the Centre for Education and Youth. https://www.sendgateway.org.uk/whole-school-send/find-wss-resources/nqt-videos.html Accessed in April 2020.

Chamberlain, S. (2020) *Demonstrating inclusion tool*. http://www.sendgateway.org.uk/download.D8D17F6E-7657-4635-B7FEBD57F9D4BCA2.html Accessed in April 2020.

CUREE (2011) *Evaluation of CPD providers in England 2010–2011: Report for school leaders*. Commissioned by the Training and Development Agency for Schools and carried out by the Centre for the Use of Research and Evidence in Education. http://www.curee.co.uk/files/publication/[site-timestamp]/CPD%20providers%20report%20-school%20leaders%20final.pdf Accessed in May 2020.

Curran, H. (2019) *How to Be a Brilliant SENCO: Practical Strategies for Developing and Leading Inclusive Provision*. Routledge: London, UK.

Curran, H., Maloney, H., Heavey, A. and Boddison, A. (2018) *It's about time: the impact of SENCO workload on the professional and the school*. https://www.bathspa.ac.uk/media/bathspaacuk/education-/research/senco-workload/SENCOWorkloadReport-FINAL2018.pdf Accessed in June 2019.

Curran, H., Maloney, H., Heavey, A. and Boddison, A. (2020) *The time is now: addressing missed opportunities for Special Educational Needs Support and Coordination in our schools*. https://www.bathspa.ac.uk/media/bathspaacuk/education-/research/senco-workload/National-SENCO-Workload-Survey-Report-Jan-2020.pdf Accessed in June 2019.

Devarakonda, C. (2013) *Diversity and Inclusion in Early Childhood: An Introduction*. Sage: London, UK.

DfE (2014) *Schools Guide to the New SEND Code of Practice: Advice for School Governing Bodies/Proprietors, Senior Leadership Teams, SENCOs and Classroom Staff*. Crown Publishing: London, UK.

DfE (2015) *Policy Paper: 2010 to 2015 government policy: Education of disadvantaged children*. https://www.gov.uk/government/publications/2010-to-2015-government-policy-education-of-disadvantaged-children/2010-to-2015-government-policy-education-of-disadvantaged-children Accessed in May 2020.

DfE (2017) *Exclusions guidance*. https://assets.publishing.service.gov.uk/government/uploads/system/uploads/attachment_data/file/641418/20170831_Exclusion_Stat_guidance_Web_version.pdf Accessed in April 2020.

DfE (2019) *School exclusions data*. https://www.gov.uk/government/collections/statistics-exclusions Accessed in April 2020.

DfE (2019a) *Governance handbook: For academies, multi-academy trusts and maintained schools*. https://assets.publishing.service.gov.uk/government/uploads/system/uploads/attachment_data/file/788234/governance_handbook_2019.pdf Accessed in May 2020.

DfE (2019b) *Pupil premium: Strategy statements*. https://www.gov.uk/guidance/pupil-premium-strategy-statements Accessed in May 2020.

DfE (2019c) *Pupil premium: Effective use and accountability*. https://www.gov.uk/guidance/pupil-premium-effective-use-and-accountability#online-statements Accessed in May 2020.

DfE (2020) *Statutory policies for schools and academy trusts*. https://www.gov.uk/government/publications/statutory-policies-for-schools-and-academy-trusts Accessed in May 2020.

DfE (2020a) *Special educational needs and disability: An analysis of summary and data sources*. May 2020. https://assets.publishing.service.gov.uk/government/uploads/system/uploads/attachment_data/file/882802/Special_educational_needs_and_disability_-_an_analysis_and_summary_of_data_sources.pdf Accessed in June 2020.

DfE (2020b) *Special educational needs in England: January 2020*. https://www.gov.uk/government/statistics/special-educational-needs-in-england-january-2020 Accessed in July 2020.

DfE (2007–2019) *Statistical releases*. https://www.gov.uk/government/collections/statistics-special-educational-needs-sen Accessed in July 2019.

DfE and DoH (2015) *SEND Code of Practice, January 2015*. https://www.gov.uk/government/publications/send-code-of-practice-0-to-25 Accessed in January 2020.

DWP and ODI (2018) *Accessible communication formats*. https://www.gov.uk/government/publications/inclusive-communication/accessible-communication-formats Accessed in February 2020.

EADSNE (2011) *Participation in Inclusive Education: A Framework for Developing Indicators*. European Agency for Development in Special Needs Education. https://www.european-agency.org/sites/default/files/participation-in-inclusive-education-a-framework-for-developing-indicators_Participation-in-Inclusive-Education.pdf Accessed in April 2020.

Early Years SEND Partnership (2019) *Early years SEND review guide*. https://www.sendgateway.org.uk/download.60374870-7798-4C6E-99383452FA15A036.html Accessed in April 2020.

Education Scotland (2019) *Inclusion in practice: The CIRCLE framework – Secondary*. https://education.gov.scot/improvement/learning-resources/inclusion-in-practice Accessed in April 2020.

EEF (2020) *Special Educational Needs in Mainstream Schools Guidance Report*. March 2020. https://educationendowmentfoundation.org.uk/public/files/Publications/Send/EEF_Special_Educational_Needs_in_Mainstream_Schools_Guidance_Report.pdf Accessed in May 2020.

Finch, P.D. (2010) Learning-walk continuum. *School Administrator*. Vol. 67, No. 10, pp 16–22.

Fisher, R., Ury, W. and Patton, B. (1999) *Negotiating an Agreement Without Giving in*. Second Edition. Random House Business Books: London, UK.

Frederickson, N. and Cline, T. (2009) *Special Educational Needs, Inclusion and Diversity*. Second Edition. Open University Press: Maidenhead, UK.

Garner, P., Hallett, F., Hallett, G. and Armstrong, D. (2019) *Warnock: 40 years on (editorial overview)*. https://onlinelibrary.wiley.com/page/journal/14679604/homepage/warnockvirtualissue Accessed in February 2020.

Gov UK (2010) *Equality Act*. http://www.legislation.gov.uk/ukpga/2010/15/contents Accessed in May 2020.

Gov UK (2014) *Children and Families Act*. http://www.legislation.gov.uk/ukpga/2014/6/contents/enacted Accessed in April 2020.

HM Government (2006) *Working together to safeguard children: A guide to inter-agency working to safeguard and promote the welfare of children*. https://www.nscb.org.uk/sites/default/files/publications/Working-Together-to-Safeguard-Children-2006_0.pdf Accessed in May 2020.

House of Commons Education Committee (2019) *Special educational needs and disabilities: First report of session 2019*. https://publications.parliament.uk/pa/cm201919/cmselect/cmeduc/20/20.pdf Accessed in June 2020.

ISC (2020) *Independent Schools Council SEND Information*. https://www.isc.co.uk/schools/sub-pages/send/ Accessed in July 2020.

Josephson, M. (2001) *You Don't Have to Be Sick to Get Better*. Josephson Institute for Ethics: California.

Killey, B. (2018) *Musical Kipper*. https://starlightmckenzie.wordpress.com/author/starlightmckenzie/ Accessed in June 2020.

Knight, S. and Busk, M. (2020) *A guide to making conversations count for all families*. https://www.sendgateway.org.uk/download.CEB5F2B8-F323-455A-800DB4A69D3552B4.html Accessed in April 2020.

Knight, S. (2020) *SEND Reflection Framework*. http://www.sendgateway.org.uk/download.F047F1C5-11A8-4506-A379503F11795921.html Accessed in April 2020.

Lamb, B. (2018) *Improving SEN support in educational settings*. Presentation for Family Voice. https://www.familyvoice.org/sites/default/files/Improving%20SEN%20Support%20in%20Educational%20Settings-Peterborough%20June%202018_0.pdf Accessed in May 2020.

Lemons, R.W. and Helsing, D. (2009) Learning to walk, walking to learn: Reconsidering the walkthrough as an improvement strategy. *Phi Delta Kappan*. Vol. 90, No. 7, pp 474–484.

Lewis, T.F. (2017) *SENCO wellbeing: A mixed methods exploration of workplace demands and effective coping actions*. Volume 1 of a thesis submitted to the University of Birmingham for the award of Applied Educational and Child Psychology Doctorate. https://etheses.bham.ac.uk/id/eprint/7781/1/Lewis17ApEd&ChildPsyD_vol_1.pdf Accessed in May 2020.

Maguire, A. (2016) *Equality, equity and liberation* https://medium.com/@CRA1G/the-evolution-of-an-accidental-meme-ddc4e139e0e4 Accessed in December 2019.

McCann, J. and McCann, E. (2004) *Inclusion quality mark*. https://iqmaward.com/ Accessed in June 2020.

McGill, R.M. (2020) *How can we reduce 'persistent disruptive behaviour' in our young people?* Teacher Toolkit. https://www.teachertoolkit.co.uk/2020/01/13/exclusions/ Accessed in July 2020.

Moloney, H. (2020) *Effective SENCO deployment*. http://www.sendgateway.org.uk/download.0432782B-F529-4221-8000D0484EEF4D5D.html Accessed in April 2020.

Moloney, H. (2020a) *Laying my ghosts to rest*. https://hannahmoloney.co.uk/blog/f/laying-my-ghosts-to-bed Accessed in August 2020.

Montgomery, D. (2015) *Teaching Gifted Children with Special Educational Needs: Supporting Dual and Multiple Exceptionality*. Routledge: London, UK.

Morewood, G. (2018) Corporate Responsibility. In Bartram, D., *Great Expectations: Leading an Effective SEND Strategy in School*. John Catt: Woodbridge.

nasen (2014) *SEN support and the graduated approach: A quick guide to ensuring that every child or young person gets the support they require to meet their needs*. https://nasen.org.uk/uploads/assets/7f6a967f-adc3-4ea9-8668320016bc5595/SENsupportpress.pdf Accessed in April 2020.

nasen and NGA (2018) *SEND governance training*. National Association for Special Educational Needs and National Governance Association: Powerpoint presentation, Accessed in March 2020.

National Audit Office (2019) *Support for pupils with special educational needs and disabilities in England*. https://www.nao.org.uk/wp-content/uploads/2019/09/Support-for-pupils-with-special-education-needs.pdf Accessed in February 2020.

NCSE (2014) *Inclusive Education Framework: A Guide for Schools on the Inclusion of Pupils with Special Educational Needs*. National Council of Special Education. https://ncse.ie/wp-content/uploads/2014/10/InclusiveEducationFramework_InteractiveVersion.pdf Accessed in April 2020.

NGA (2020) National Governance Association. https://www.nga.org.uk/Home.aspx Accessed in March 2020.

NHS England (2017) *Accessible information standard*. https://www.england.nhs.uk/ourwork/accessibleinfo/ Accessed in May 2020.

Norwich, B. and Jones, J. (2014) *Lesson Study: Making a Difference to Teaching Pupils with Learning Difficulties*. Bloomsbury: London, UK.

Nrich (2020) *Noah*. https://nrich.maths.org/136/note Accessed in April 2020.

Ofsted (2010) *The special educational needs and disability review: A statement is not enough*. https://assets.publishing.service.gov.uk/government/uploads/system/uploads/attachment_data/file/413814/Special_education_needs_and_disability_review.pdf Accessed in November 2019.

Ofsted (2012) *The pupil premium: How schools are using the pupil premium funding to raise achievement for disadvantaged pupils*. https://assets.publishing.service.gov.uk/government/uploads/system/uploads/attachment_data/file/413222/The_Pupil_Premium.pdf Accessed in May 2020.

Ofsted (2013) *The pupil premium: How schools are spending the funding successfully*. https://www.gov.uk/government/publications/the-pupil-premium-how-schools-are-spending-the-funding-successfully Accessed May 2020.

Ofsted (2014) *Pupil premium: Update on school's progress*. https://www.gov.uk/government/publications/the-pupil-premium-an-update Accessed in May 2020.

Ofsted (2019) *Off-rolling*. https://www.gov.uk/government/publications/off-rolling-exploring-the-issue Accessed in May 2020.

Ofsted (2019a) *The Education Inspection Framework*. https://assets.publishing.service.gov.uk/government/uploads/system/uploads/attachment_data/file/801429/Education_inspection_framework.pdf Accessed in January 2020.

Ofsted (2019b) *The School Inspection Handbook*. https://assets.publishing.service.gov.uk/government/uploads/system/uploads/attachment_data/file/801429/Education_inspection_framework.pdf Accessed in January 2020.

Packer, N. (2014) *The Perfect SENCO*. Independent Thinking Press: Wales.

Parker, B. and Bowell, B. (1998) Exploiting computer-mediated communication support in-service professional development: The SENCO experience. *Journal of Information Technology for Teacher Education*. Vol. 7, No. 2, pp 229–246.

Pickell, D. (2019) *Qualitative vs quantitative data – What's the difference?* https://learn.g2.com/qualitative-vs-quantitative-data Accessed in March 2020.

Pillay, H., Carrington, S., Duke, J., Chandra, S., Heeraman, J., Tones, M. and Joseph, R.M. (2015) *Mobilising school and community engagement to implement disability-inclusive education through action research: Fiji, Samoa, Solomon Islands and Vanuatu*. https://core.ac.uk/download/pdf/33501783.pdf Accessed in June 2020.

Poortvliet, M., Axford, N. and Lloyd, J. (2018) *Working with parents to support children's learning*. Guidance Report published by the Education Endowment Foundation. https://educationendowmentfoundation.org.uk/public/files/Publications/ParentalEngagement/EEF_Parental_Engagement_Guidance_Report.pdf Accessed in September 2019.

Purdy, N. and Boddison, A. (2018) Special Educational Needs and Inclusion. In Cremin, T. and Burnett, C., *Learning to Teach in the Primary School*. Routledge: London, UK.

Reeve, M. (2016) *Where are we now with special needs*. In Schools Week (5th July 2016) https://schoolsweek.co.uk/where-are-we-now-with-special-needs Accessed in June 2018.

Reeve, M. (2020) *MAT SEND review guide*. http://www.sendgateway.org.uk/download.522EC46E-FD54-4B39-87BD178CAFBF649B.html Accessed in April 2020.

Reeve, M. and Packer, N. (2017) *SEND reforms – Spirit and letter*. Pearson Breakfast Meeting. https://www.pearsonclinical.co.uk/Sitedownloads/malcolm-reeve-cognition-and-learning.pdf Accessed in May 2020.

Rice-Oxley, M. (2017) *Change your mind –It's a sign of strength not weakness*. In The Guardian (20th December 2017) https://www.theguardian.com/commentisfree/2017/dec/20/change-your-mind-social-media-jeremy-corbyn Accessed in April 2020.

RNIB (2017) *Top tips for creating accessible print documents*. https://www.rnib.org.uk/sites/default/files/Top_Tips_Creating_accessible_print_documents.pdf Accessed in May 2020.

Robson, C. (2002) *Real World Research*. Second Edition. Blackwell: London, UK.

Rossiter, C. (2020) *SEND governance review guide. http://www.sendgateway.org.uk/download.AE2AEEFD-B477-4735-8A32EA5508409DFE.html* Accessed in April 2020.

Rustemier, S. (2002) *Social and Educational Justice: The Human Rights Framework for Inclusion*. Centre for Studies in Inclusive Education: Bristol.

Ryan, A. and Waterman, C. (2018) *Dual and multiple exceptionality: The current state of play*. http://www.nasen.org.uk/utilities/download.5ED13CB8-C8CD-4598-AF82808652F25719.html Accessed in September 2019.

Sayre, A.P. and Sayre, J. (2003) *One Is a Snail, Ten Is a Crab – A Counting by Feet Book*. Candlewick Press: Massachusetts.

Schwartz, M.S. (2017) *Business Ethics: An Ethical Decision-Making Approach*. Wiley Blackwell: New Jersey.

Sharples, J., Webster, R. and Blatchford, P. (2018) *Making the best use of teaching assistants*. EEF Guidance Report. https://educationendowmentfoundation.org.uk/public/files/Publications/Teaching_Assistants/TA_Guidance_Report_MakingBestUseOfTeachingAssistants-Printable.pdf Accessed in June 2020.

Silverman, L. (2013) *Giftedness 101*. Springer: Berlin, Germany.

Skretta, J. (2007) Using walk-throughs to gather data for school improvement. *Principal Leadership*. Vol. 7, No. 9, pp 16–23.

Soan, S. (2017) *The SENCO Essential Manual*. Open University Press: Maidenhead.

STEC (2014) *A National Framework for Inclusion in Education in Scotland*. Scottish Teacher Education Committee. http://www.frameworkforinclusion.org/STEC14%20Report%20Jun(PDF%20V).pdf Accessed in April 2020.

Stobbs, P., Shaw, B. and Thakore, J. (2018) *Preparing for adulthood from the earliest years review guide*. https://www.sendgateway.org.uk/download.8EB0CE4A-8ECC-4B7D-B3F3BE7C0DDAF5F2.html Accessed in April 2020.

Swaithes, L., Dziedzic, K., Sharp, C.A., Ellis, B. and Walsh, N. (2020) *Context, context, context: How has Covid-19 changed implementation globally and how can we 'lock in' learning?* Rheumatology keaa387. https://doi.org/10.1093/rheumatology/keaa387 Accessed in July 2020.

TDT (2012) *Leading CPD effectively*. Article written by David Weston of the Teacher Development Trust, published in *SMT Magazine* on 11th May 2012. https://www.smtmagazine.co.uk/leading-cpd-effectively/ Accessed in January 2020.

The Telegraph (2013) *Ofsted: 'Significant minority of schools wasting pupil premium'*. https://www.telegraph.co.uk/education/educationnews/9860603/Ofsted-signifiant-minority-of-schools-wasting-pupil-premium.html Accessed in May 2020.

The Telegraph (2014) *Ofsted: Top schools 'downgraded' for failing poor pupils*. https://www.telegraph.co.uk/education/educationnews/10968611/Ofsted-top-schools-downgraded-for-failing-poor-pupils.html Accessed in May 2020.

Timpson (2019) *Review of school exclusion*. https://assets.publishing.service.gov.uk/government/uploads/system/uploads/attachment_data/file/807862/Timpson_review.pdf Accessed in April 2020.

Tirraoro, T. (2018) *Exclusions 2018: Children with SEND Six Times More Likely to Be Excluded*. Special Needs Jungle. https://www.specialneedsjungle.com/exclusions-2018-children-with-send-six-times-more-likely-to-be-excluded/ Accessed in January 2020.

Turner, D. (2015) Globalisation, Education and Policy Research. In Zajda, J., *Second International Handbook on Globalisation, Education and Policy Research*. Springer: Berlin, Germany.

Tutt, R. (2016) *Rona Tutt's Guide to SEND and Inclusion*. Sage: London, UK.

UCL CIE and Firmament Education (2019) *Whole School SEND Index: An analysis of SEND data nationally and by Regional School Commissioner Region*. Written by University College London Centre for Inclusive Education and Firmament Education. Published by Whole School SEND and nasen. file:///C:/Users/adamb/Downloads/wss_send_index_june_2019.pdf Accessed in April 2020.

UNESCO (1994) Salamanca Statement https://unesdoc.unesco.org/ark:/48223/pf0000098427 Accessed in March 2020.

United Nations (1989) *Convention on the Rights of the Child*. https://www.unicef.org.uk/what-we-do/un-convention-child-rights Accessed in January 2020.

United Nations (2006) *Convention on the Rights of Persons with Disabilities*. https://www.un.org/development/desa/disabilities/convention-on-the-rights-of-persons-with-disabilities.html Accessed in January 2020.

United Nations (2015) *Sustainable Development Goals 2030*. https://www.un.org/development/desa/disabilities/envision2030.html Accessed in January 2020.

Warnock, M. (1978) *The Warnock Report*. http://www.educationengland.org.uk/documents/warnock/warnock1978.html Accessed in November 2019.

Warnock, M. (2019) *Warnock: 40 years on (SEN: The past and the future)*. https://onlinelibrary.wiley.com/pb-assets/assets/14679604/1.%20WARNOCK-1540389396170.pdf Accessed in February 2020.

Webster, R. (2020) *TA deployment review guide*. http://www.sendgateway.org.uk/download.997E4F77-090C-4AC0-8C55BB0E0E5F1631.html Accessed in April 2020.

Wharton, J., Codina, G., Middleton, T. and Esposita, R. (2019) *SENCO induction pack*. https://www.sendgateway.org.uk/download.1E603981-E111-4A8F-A352DF7E58519B8D.html Accessed in April 2020.

Whole School SEND (2020) *Condition specific videos*. https://www.sendgateway.org.uk/whole-school-send/find-wss-resources/nqt-videos.html Accessed in June 2020.

Woodley, H. (2017) *Should all SENCOs be an integral part of the senior leadership team?* Blog published by Teacher Toolkit. https://www.teachertoolkit.co.uk/2017/03/05/senco/ Accessed in April 2020.

Yates, D. and Boddison, A. (2020) *The School Handbook for Dual and Multiple Exceptionality: High Learning Potential with Special Educational Needs or Disabilities*. Routledge: London, UK.

Appendix 1

Practical resources and useful organisations

Provider	*Summary of resources*	*Link*

SEND Gateway	• Whole School SEND Review Suite
	  ○ Whole School SEND Review Guide
	  ○ Demonstrating Inclusion Tool
	  ○ Effective SENCO Deployment
	  ○ Preparing for Adulthood from the Earliest Years Review Guide
	  ○ SEND Reflection Framework
	  ○ Teaching Assistant Deployment Review Guide
	  ○ MAT SEND Review Guide
	  ○ Early Years SEND Review Guide
	  ○ SEND Governance Review Guide
	• A guide to making conversations count for all families (National Health Service; ask, listen and do)
	• Condition-specific videos
	  ○ ADHD
	  ○ Acquired brain injury
	  ○ Autism
	  ○ Down's syndrome
	  ○ Dyscalculia
	  ○ Dyslexia
	  ○ Dyspraxia
	  ○ Hearing impairment
	  ○ Physical disability
	  ○ SEMH
	  ○ Speech, language and communication
	  ○ Visual impairment
	• SEND Forums
	• SEND research videos and reports
	• SENCO research
	• Subject-specific SEND resources
	• SEND resources from across the sector
		www.sendgateway.org.uk

nasen	• Free *nasen* membership
	• *nasen* mini guides
	  ○ Understanding inclusion
	  ○ Improving health care: Learning disabilities and autism
	  ○ Understanding the eye care and vision needs of pupils with SEND
	  ○ Acquired brain injury: The hidden disability
	  ○ Children with medical needs: What schools and settings need to know?
	  ○ Identifying and supporting children with SEND in the early years
	  ○ Girls and autism: Flying under the radar
	  ○ The SEND Code of Practice: 0–25 years
	  ○ Supporting pupils with specific learning difficulties
		www.nasen.org.uk

(*Continued*)

Provider	*Summary of resources*	*Link*
	o Effective adult support o SEN Support and the graduated approach o Working in partnership with parents and carers o The pupil premium o Tracking progress and managing provision o Transition o Supporting reading and literacy in secondary schools • *nasen* journals o JORSEN: Journal of Research in Special Educational Needs o BJSE: British Journal of Special Education o SfL: Support for Learning • SEND training and CPD • SEND webinars and webcasts • Templates and resources for SENCOs and SEND Governors • Early years resources • Youth mental health first aid courses • National professional qualification in senior leadership (with a focus on SEND and inclusion) • SEND Casework Award • Recognised teacher/practitioner of SEND • *nasen* Live Annual Conference and *nasen* Awards • Spotlight book series (published by Routledge) • SENCO Support Service	
NGA (National Governance Association)	• Articles on SEND and SEND governance • Guidance for SEND Governors • Knowledge Centre, including pupil success and wellbeing	www.nga.org.uk
The Key	• Podcasts, articles and case studies on SEND • Key questions on SEND answered	www.thekeysupport.com
UK Government	• National Leaders of Governance • SEND statistics • Official SEND publications and guidance documents • Ofsted	www.gov.uk
Other SEND/ Specialist Organisations	• ADHD Foundation • Anna Freud National Centre for Children and Families • Autism Education Trust • Axcis • British Association for Supported Employment • British Dyslexia Association	www.adhdfoundation.org.uk www.annafreud.org www.autismeducationtrust.org.uk www.axcis.co.uk www.base-UK.org www.bdadyslexia.org.uk
(NB – There are many hundreds of organisations and not all could be included here. This list is provided as a useful starting point for governors)	• British Stammering Association • Centre for Education and Youth • Council for Disabled Children • Contact • Down's Syndrome Association • Dyslexia SpLD Trust • Dyspraxia Foundation • Driver Youth Trust • Equals • GL Assessment • ICAN • IPSEA • KIDS • Jelly James • Leading Learning for SEND Community Interest Company • Makaton	www.stamma.org www.cfey.org www.councilfordisabledchildren.org.uk www.contact.org.uk www.downs-syndrome.org.uk www.thedyslexia-spldtrust.org.uk www.dyspraxiafoundation.org.uk www.driveryouthtrust.com www.equals.co.uk www.gl-assessment.co.uk www.ican.org.uk www.ipsea.org.uk www.kids.org.uk

Provider	Summary of resources	Link
	• MindEd	www.jellyjames.co.uk
	• NASS	www.nasenco.org.uk
	• NatiSIP	www.makaton.org
	• National Children's Bureau	www.minded.org.uk
	• National Deaf Children's Society	www.nasschools.org.uk
	• NDTi	www.natsip.org.uk
	• Nisai Learning	www.ncb.org.uk
	• NNPCF	www.ndcs.org.uk
	• PDnet	www.ndti.org.uk
	• Place2Be	www.nisai.com
	• Potential Plus UK	www.nnpcf.org.uk
	• Real Training	www.pdnet.org.uk
	• RNIB	www.place2be.org.uk
	• SeeAbility	www.potentialplusuk.org
	• SMIRA	www.realtraining.co.uk
	• Special Needs Jungle	www.rnib.org.uk
	• UCL Centre for Inclusive Education	www.seeability.org
	• UK Acquired Brain Injury Forum	www.selectivemutism.org.uk
	• University of Wolverhampton Education Observatory	www.specialneedsjungle.com
	• Young Epilepsy	www.ucl.ac.uk/ioe/departments-and-centres/centres/ucl-centre-inclusive-education
	• Youth Sport Trust	www.ukabif.org.uk
		www.wlv.ac.uk/research/institutes-and-centres/education-observatory
		www.youngepilepsy.org.uk
		www.youthsporttrust.org

Appendix 2

Summary of the 50 key messages

1. The school environment is a key factor in the identification of SEND.
2. The social model of SEND is focused on removing barriers to learning in the environment.
3. Effective practice for learners with SEND is often effective practice for all learners.
4. Value a broad notion of outcomes.
5. Ensure that learners with SEND are not excluded from school because of behaviours due to unmet needs.
6. The graduated approach of 'assess, plan, do, review' should be used to develop effective provision.
7. The vast majority of pupils with SEND are at the SEN support level.
8. Coproduction is essential for SEND provision to be effective.
9. The concept of inclusion is complex and there is limited consensus on how it is achieved in practice.
10. SEND and HLP can co-occur and this is known as DME.
11. All governors, trustees and school leaders should be familiar with Chapter 6 of the SEND Code of Practice (DfE and DoH, 2015).
12. Give SEND the same status as pupil premium.
13. Ensure that all governors and trustees have access to specialist knowledge and information in relation to SEND and inclusion.
14. Every leader a leader of SEND.
15. Think SEND!
16. Coproduction is an essential feature of effective SEND governance.
17. Governors should use data to inform strategic decision-making.
18. Governors should have a common understanding of SEND and inclusion for the specific context of their school.
19. Ethical leadership is a key feature of effective SEND governance.
20. A high-quality SEN Information Report will support both school staff and families.
21. Effective governance is more about the journey than the destination.
22. Effective governance is directly related to effective SEND governance.
23. A review of SEND governance can provide essential intelligence to inform a governance action plan.
24. The Whole School SEND suite of review guides are frameworks for critical reflection and strategic planning, not a simple checklist of compliance.
25. Effective reviews of SEND provision and SEND governance draw on elements of self-evaluation, peer review and external review.
26. Learning walks can be a catalyst for purposeful professional discussion in the board room.
27. SEND learning walks reinforce the principle that SEND is the responsibility of all governors.
28. SEND learning walks can develop governors' knowledge of SEND.
29. Governors should be both proactive and reactive when asking questions about SEND.
30. Governors should ensure they have access to ongoing professional support in relation to SEND governance.
31. The SEND Governor is not personally responsible or accountable for the school's provision for learners with SEND.
32. The SEND Governor is a critical friend to the SENCO – not their line manager.
33. The SENCO is most effective when they are part of the school leadership team (DfE and DoH, 2015, p108).
34. The Director of Inclusion role in a MAT is most effective when it is in addition to, and not instead of, SENCOs in individual schools.
35. SENCOs should be spending the vast majority of their time on strategic rather than operational matters.
36. There is no requirement for special schools to have a SENCO or a SEND Governor, but when they do they should be appropriately qualified.

37. The SEND Governor should ensure that coproduction is happening and that it is effective.
38. The SEND Governor should meet at least termly with the SENCO.
39. School leaders and SENCOs should aim for at least 40% of staff training and professional development to be SEND-related (Morewood, 2018, p 19).
40. The SEND Governor should support the SENCO to produce an annual SEND report for governors.
41. Governors should ensure there is a shared notion of what inclusion means for their school.
42. There is no one metric for measuring inclusion.
43. High levels of unauthorised absence amongst pupils with SEND should be explored by governors.
44. Boards should know what actions they can take to support the removal of barriers and challenges for learners with SEND.
45. Governors should consider school data in the context of local and national data.
46. School data should always be considered in the context of feedback from families, not in isolation.
47. Governors should use data on the physical school environment as an opportunity to champion greater inclusion.
48. Governors should ensure there is value for money on SEND spend.
49. Battles should be small enough to win, but big enough to make a difference.
50. Ultimately, governors should ensure that ‘no child is missed’ and that ‘no child misses out’ (Moloney, 2020a).

Appendix 3

Glossary of acronyms

ADHD	Attention deficit hyperactivity disorder
ALN	Additional learning needs
AP	Alternative provision
ARP	Additionally resourced provision
ASN	Additional support needs
BSL	British sign language
CBT	Cognitive behavioural therapy
DME	Dual or multiple exceptionality
DSG	Dedicated Schools Grant
EEF	Education Endowment Foundation
EHC plan	Education, Health and Care plan
EP	Education psychologist
GDPR	General Data Protection Regulations
HLP	High learning potential
HI	Hearing impairment
JCQ	Joint Council for Qualifications
LD	Learning disabilities
LO	Local Offer
MAT	Multi-academy trust
MLD	Moderate learning difficulties
MSI	Multi-sensory impairment
nasen	National Association for Special Educational Needs
NASENCO	National Award for Special Educational Needs Coordination
NGA	National Governance Association
OP	Occupational therapist
PD	Physical disability
PfA	Preparation for adulthood
PMLD	Profound and multiple learning difficulties
PRU	Pupil referral unit
QfT	Quality-first teaching
RNIB	Royal National Institute for the Blind
SaLT	Speech and language therapist
SEMH	Social, emotional and mental health needs
SEN	Special educational needs
SENCO	Special educational needs coordinator
SEND	Special educational needs and/or disabilities
SLCN	Speech, language and communication needs
SLD	Severe learning difficulties
SpLD	Specific learning difficulties

STA	Standards and Testing Agency
TA	Teaching assistant
TDT	Teacher Development Trust
VI	Vision impairment
WSS	Whole School SEND
2E	Twice exceptional

Index

Note: *Italicized* pages refer to figures and pages in bold refer to tables.